MW00527724

SECRET
GLASGOW

Stephen Millar and Gillian Loney

JONGLEZ PUBLISHING

Travel guides

Stephen Millar was born and brought up in Glasgow and now splits his time between there and Edinburgh. He has long had an interest in urban exploration and takes walking groups around Glasgow, Edinburgh, and London. His articles and photographs have appeared in iNews, The Scotsman, The Herald on Sunday, Edinburgh Evening News, Edinburgh Live, and The Daily Record. Stephen has spoken about his book Tribes of Glasgow at Glasgow's Aye Write! Book Festival.

Gillian Loney is a journalist, columnist and editor of Glasgow Live, the city's biggest news website. She has spent a decade covering culture, what's on and breaking news, and specialises in writing about Glasgow's growing food and drink scene – which means she's always on hand to recommend local restaurants. Her work has also featured in the *Daily Record*, *The Scotsman*, the *Daily Mirror*, the Wow24–7 website and more. *Secret Glasgow*, her first book, marks a new chapter for her.

W e have taken great pleasure in drawing up *Secret Glasgow* and hope that through its guidance you will, like us, continue to discover unusual, hidden or little-known aspects of the city.

Descriptions of certain places are accompanied by thematic sections highlighting historical details or anecdotes as an aid to understanding the city in all its complexity. *Secret Glasgow* also draws attention to the multitude of details found in places that we may pass every day without noticing.

These are an invitation to look more closely at the urban landscape and, more generally, a means of seeing our own region with the curiosity and attention that we often display while travelling elsewhere ...

Comments on this guidebook and its contents, as well as information on places we may not have mentioned, are more than welcome and will enrich future editions.

Don't hesitate to contact us:
E-mail: info@jonglezpublishing.com
Jonglez Publishing, 25 rue du Maréchal Foch
78000 Versailles, France

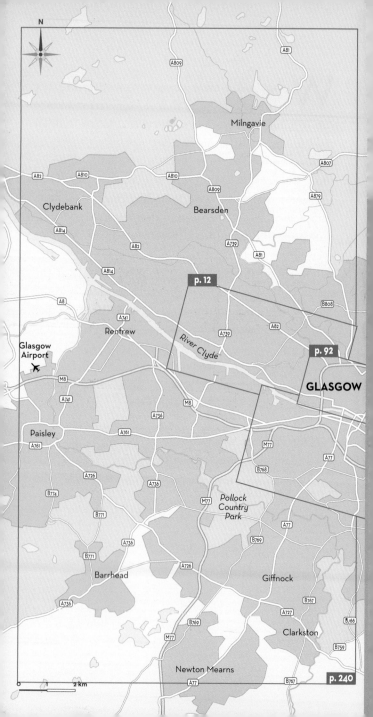

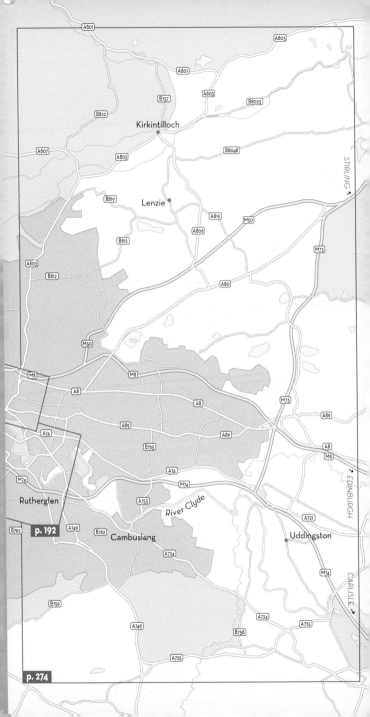

p. 192

p. 274

CONTENTS

Glasgow West

Glasgow Centre

CONTENTS

Glasgow South

Glasgow - To the West and South

Glasgow - To the North and East

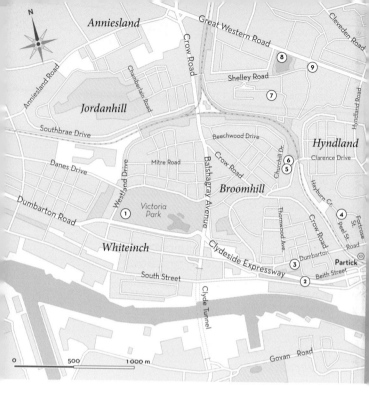

Glasgow West

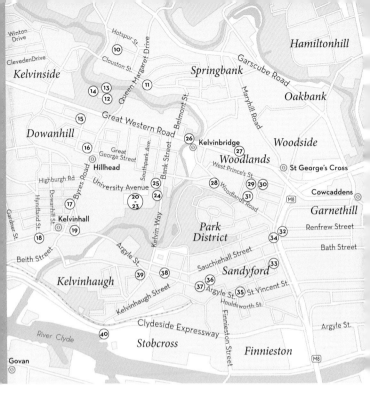

FOSSIL GROVE

A unique find the world over ...

51 Victoria Park Drive South, G14 9QR
0141 287 5918
fossilgroveglasgow.org
April–October: Saturday & Sunday noon–4pm
Free
Partick Subway/train/bus station
Buses for Whiteinch and Scotstoun, Jordanhill station

In the west end of the city, at Victoria Park, Glasgow has its very own prehistoric attraction, a fascinating slice of history from long before the city even existed.

The leafy park was being constructed in 1887, with workmen cutting a path through an old disused quarry, when the first fossil tree stump was uncovered. They went on to find 10 more, each around 330 million years old, perfectly preserved on the spot they once grew, long before there were men, let alone fishermen, to settle on the banks of the Clyde. In fact, long before the British Isles were here too ...

Dating from the Carboniferous Period, the 11 tree stumps are regarded as a unique find the world over. Park planners quickly recognised their importance and incorporated them into the park as a star attraction, constructing a building around the site which still stands today. The place became popular with Victorian and Edwardian tourists visiting Glasgow: the website run by the Fossil Trust has some fascinating postcards of the place which prove its popularity at the time.

Today, the site is still owned and operated by Glasgow City Council, with help from the trust. The quarry is there too, providing a rocky walkway to the west end of the park: perfect if you're taking a stroll on a sunny day.

There has been much debate about how best to put the site on the map, with few Glaswegians knowing about Fossil Grove, never mind visitors. Some people have suggested broadening its appeal by linking it with the ongoing fascination for dinosaurs and prehistoric creatures; others have rejected that in favour of more scientific displays. Plans have been drawn up to revamp the Victorian structure standing over the fossil stumps – so it could yet be turned into an attraction to rival others in the city.

In the meantime, if you're looking for a flashy, all-singing, all-dancing museum, you're out of luck. Little has changed at Fossil Grove in the last century.

RISE SCULPTURE

Stunning sculpture by the man who created
The Kelpies

Between Castlebank Street and Glasgow Harbour Terraces, G11 6BS
Partick Subway station

The famous *Kelpies* at Falkirk are the work of sculptor Andy Scott, a graduate of the Glasgow School of Art. They have become arguably the best-known example of public art in Scotland. However, there is another striking example of Scott's work just a stone's throw from the Clyde beside a busy roadway.

A little out of central Glasgow, *Rise* is a stunning sculpture standing 6 metres tall. Made in 2008, it is a piece of public art that deserves to be better known.

According to Scott: 'She was commissioned by Peel Holdings, the owners of Glasgow Harbour. My inspiration was the old shipyards and docks of the Clyde. Her "wings" are shaped like ship's propellers and the steel segments of her construction spiral upwards. I wanted to try and create something emblematic which might represent the regeneration of the riverside area. I also made a cast bronze maquette of the sculpture which is 60 cm tall. The sculpture created an instant positive reaction with the client and subsequently seems to have been very well received by the local residents at Glasgow Harbour. The client wanted something that might create a human element within that linear parkway that runs along South Street, and apparently she fulfils that role well.'

Made in Scott's studio in Maryhill, *Rise* was made in two sections, bolted together around 'her' waist. The sculpture was unveiled in 2008.

WESTER SPIRIT CO. RUM DISTILLERY

A city rife with rum production, thanks to a boom in the sugar industry

Unit 2, 8 Meadow Road, G11 6HX
Saturday & Sunday, noon–4pm
Tours: book on website westerspirit.com
Partick Subway, train or bus station

When the Clydeside distillery (see p. 88) was launched in 2017, much was said about whisky production returning to Glasgow. Little do many drinkers know that the city was once famous for another liquor – at once more exotic, and yet so familiar to us too. Enter Wester Spirit Co., a distillery bringing rum production back to the heart of Scotland for the first time in more than 300 years. The place was established in a side street off Partick's busy Dumbarton Road in 2018, and today you'll find more and more bars stocking Wester rum.

For most people, the spirit may be associated more closely with the swaying palm trees of the Caribbean than with rainy Glasgow – but if you were to travel back several centuries, you would find a city rife with rum production, thanks to a boom in the sugar industry. Prosperous Glasgow

merchants were importing the stuff, along with tobacco, from far-off Jamaica. They were also using profits from the slave trade to fund some of the more elaborate city architecture celebrated today – the most famous example being the Gallery of Modern Art, once the Cunninghame mansion built on West Indies sugar. Between 1650 and 1750, most of the city's sugar refineries would have housed a rum distillery too … questionable origins or not, it's fair to say that rum was once a booming business in Glasgow.

West-coast-born founders Zander Macgregor and Allan Nairn shared an interest in rum and small batch craft spirits, experimenting with the distilling process in Strathearn before expanding to the busy west end of Glasgow. The name is a homage to the Wester sugar house, once located at Candleriggs, but today, you'll find Wester Spirit Co. in Meadow Road. And, like any good distillery, you're welcome to take a tour of the place. There, you can get up close and personal with the stainless-steel stills (a step away from conventional copper), take a masterclass in the history of rum and the making of it today, not to mention mix your own Wester cocktail.

Still relatively new to the city, the place remains a hidden gem except for those in the know about their small batch spirits – but it's well worth the subway fare to Partick and the entry fee for a taste of something sweet and tropical, as well as a lesson in forgotten Glasgow history.

WEST OF SCOTLAND CRICKET CLUB ④

Glasgow's oldest cricketing institution

Hamilton Crescent, 40–44 Peel Street, G11 5LU
westofscotlandcricketclub.co.uk
Kelvinhall or Partick Subway station

Ahigh fence around the West of Scotland Cricket Club in Partick helps hide this sporting institution even from local residents, and surprisingly few Glaswegians are aware of their city's thriving cricket scene.

Compared to football, cricket is regarded by many Scots as a minority sport, associated with being an 'English' rather than a Scottish pastime. However, it has more regular players in Scotland than rugby union, and cricket has been played in Glasgow since the 19th century.

The West of Scotland Cricket Club has been the leading centre for this sport since 1862, when it was founded by businessmen and players who were already associated with the Clutha Cricket Club.

The meeting to found the new club took place at a hotel in George Square – the club was expected to become the leading institution in Scotland, the equivalent of the MCC in England. In those days, the West of Scotland regularly played top English teams and even a team of Australians in 1878. The famous amateur cricketer W. G. Grace played with a team here in 1891.

The club's glory years were in the early 1920s, when it had over 500 members and its ground could hold up to 3,500 spectators: that number came to watch Scotland play Australia at the club's ground in 1989.

There is also a football connection with the club as the first international match between Scotland and England took place here in 1872. The club also claims to be the only sports ground in the UK to have hosted international games of cricket, rugby union, football and hockey.

Whisper it quietly, but in the 1930s many Rangers fans used to watch cricket here when the football season was over – not something that many Glaswegians would expect to see today.

There around 17 other cricket clubs in the Glasgow area, including Clydesdale, Poloc, Glasgow Accies, GHK and Drumpellier.

In recent years, the West of Scotland Club has introduced a women's team in response to a growth in the popularity of women's cricket in Scotland.

If you want to watch a game, look at the club's website for the fixture list – games are normally held on Saturdays and Sundays and the season starts at the end of April and runs until the first week in September. The club is currently on the lookout for new players. See the contact details on their website.

RELICS OF CROW ROAD RAILWAY STATION ⑤

'Ghost' platforms of a defunct railway line

Clarence Gardens, G11 7JN
Hyndland train station

If you walk along Clarence Gardens, a quiet suburban street, and look through some overgrown bushes near the end, you can see an abandoned railway platform covered in litter and hidden by a road bridge above. This is all that remains of Crow Road station, one of several ghostly reminders in Glasgow of an age when ambitious railway companies opened up station after station and the possibilities of further expansion seemed endless.

Old maps of Glasgow show the mass of railway lines, stations and tunnels that used to snake across the city but were later closed down and demolished or abandoned. However, if you know where to look, you can see dozens of ghostly relics of the railway age in Scotland.

The derelict platform shown in the picture is one of them. It was initially part of the Lanarkshire and Dumbartonshire Railway (L&DR) that opened in 1896. The L&DR was taken over by the much larger Caledonian Railway in 1909.

In its heyday, the L&DR connected Dumbarton with Glasgow, operating right along the north side of the Clyde, where many heavy industries and shipyards were based. Industrialists used the line to move their heavy goods while thousands of ordinary workers relied on the L&DR for their daily commute.

The L&DR and other privately owned railways had sprung up to meet a demand in Glasgow and so their fortunes were closely connected to the industries and workers who used them. As the city's heavy industries, particularly shipbuilding, began to decline in the years after the Second World War, the railways that grew up in their shadow struggled to justify their existence. The nationalisation of the railway system and the growth of road traffic led to many other smaller, uneconomic routes being closed down. This left dozens of ghost stations stranded in urban areas.

Crow Road was just one of the many victims of Glasgow's decline, closing in 1960. The empty station building survived another ten years and now only the remains of the original platform – previously open to the air – remain.

SARACEN FOUNTAIN

A legacy of the Glasgow International Exhibition of 1901

Alexandra Park, G31 3LJ
Alexandra Parade train station

In Alexandra Park stands the magnificent Saracen Fountain, constructed in 1901 by Walter Macfarlane & Co. It was originally made as the company's main exhibit at the Glasgow International Exhibition held in Kelvingrove Park in 1901.

The exhibition boasted a Grand Avenue, an Industrial Hall, various pavilions sponsored by commercial concerns and exhibits from around the world. Charles Rennie Mackintosh submitted plans for the overall design but these were rejected in favour of those by another well-known Glaswegian architect, James Miller.

The Saracen Fountain was gifted to the city by its manufacturer after the exhibition ended and it remained in Kelvingrove Park for several years before being moved to its present location in 1914.

Why was it named the Saracen Fountain? Macfarlane & Co's first foundry in the 1850s was set up in Saracen Lane in Gallowgate, right

behind the famous Saracen Head Inn. A much larger site was later built in Possil but was still known as the Saracen works. From here the firm produced decorative ironwork, ranging from street lamps and bandstands to railings and fountains. It became the leading manufacturer of its kind in Scotland and employed the best available talent, including the renowned architect, Alexander 'Greek' Thomson.

Designed by David Watson Stevenson, the Saracen Fountain has an astonishing amount of detail, with four classical maidens representing Literature, Science, Art and Commerce. Look for the lion and dolphin mask waterspouts, signs of the zodiac, seashells and cherubs.

Macfarlane's operated from the mid-1850s until it was taken over in the 1960s and the main site in Possil closed. However, reminders of this once-famous Glasgow firm can be seen around the world in countries such as India, Canada, Brazil, Argentina, Cyprus, South Africa and Australia. The Saracen Fountain remains its most celebrated work and featured heavily in the firm's advertising.

If you're in Pretoria, South Africa, you might want to visit the Sammy Marks Fountain in the National Zoological Gardens – it's a copy of the Saracen Fountain.

> The only other substantive remains of the 1901 Exhibition are the two Port Sunlight cottages that still stand in the grounds of Kelvingrove Park.

GARTNAVEL HOSPITAL GARDEN ⑦

A magical healing space

Gartnavel Royal Hospital
1055 Great Western Road, G12 0XH
Gartnavel Royal Hospital Volunteers: 07977 406900
Open 24/7

Most people only visit a hospital such as Gartnavel because they have to. However, it contains one of the city's most hidden treasures: a beautiful walled garden that is open to the public.

This horticultural delight is tucked away on the hospital's 27-hectare estate, a few minutes' walk on the west side of the main entrance by Great Western Road. It was first laid out in the 1830s, when it was used by the hospital's superintendent. It was restored a few years ago by a group of dedicated volunteers.

The walled garden features hundreds of medicinal and sensory plants grown on organic principles. It is split into three areas. The first (as you enter) is the 'physic garden', where plants used for healing purposes are grown. These include feverfew for headaches and yarrow for colds – a continuation of the historic tradition of physic gardens being founded by medical establishments.

The next area is the cottage garden, which features edible plants such as rhubarb and salad crops. This continues another tradition as, until the 1960s, the hospital had a working farm that provided food for the hospital kitchen. The last part of the walled garden is a wildlife area.

Beside the garden is a greenhouse (known as the Summerhouse), which is also used for art workshops and as a performance space for music. Many decades ago, the medical staff at the hospital pioneered the idea of encouraging patients suffering from mental illness to work in the garden or just sit in the sun.

Today this 'secret garden' and the surrounding green space is a lovely spot used by patients, visitors and staff. It is open all the time but is often empty as so few people know about it.

If you would like to volunteer at the garden, phone the contact number given above.

BINGHAM'S POND

An often-overlooked oasis

Near 1057 Great Western Rd, G12 0XP
Anniesland or Hyndland train station
Bus: 6

Sandwiched between the busy Great Western Road and Gartnavel General Hospital, Bingham's Pond is popular with locals but rarely visited by Glaswegians living further afield. That's a shame as it's a beautiful place.

Surprisingly, its origins were less auspicious: the pond was created over some abandoned coal and brick pits in the 1880s. A boathouse was later built and three generations of the Bingham family provided skating and boating facilities in the late 19th century – hence the pond's name.

In the late 1940s a young Billy Connolly used to come here regularly to sail his beloved toy yacht on the pond, a present from his father on his return from the war.

A large part of the pond was built over for a car park and hotel development in the 1960s, and the area became run-down and unloved. Recently, however, a major project created two islands with thousands of new plants. Swans, mallards and moorhens began to nest on the islands, creating a new wildlife centre in a heavily built-up part of the city.

What remains has become popular with swans and other wildlife, all in the shadow of Gartnavel General Hospital. It's a great place for a picnic and you can find wild blackberries and cherries here.

'CR' INSCRIPTION

Traces of the former Caledonian Railway

1051 Great Western Road, G12 0XP
Hyndland train station
Buses: 6, 6A

An Italianate Victorian villa on the Great Western Road might not seem very unusual in Glasgow ... perhaps just another elegant house converted into a restaurant. However, if you get close on the north side and look up, you will see the intertwined letters 'CR'. If you walk to the back of the building, you can peer through fencing into a ghostly tunnel underneath and see the marks on the exterior walls indicating where the staircase down to the railway platforms used to run.

The letters stand for the Caledonian Railway: this was once one of the grandest suburban railway stations in Glasgow. Its architect, Sir John James Burnet (1857–1938), was also responsible for much better-known structures in the city such as the Clydeport Building.

Burnet's building was designed as the Kelvinside train station, which opened in 1897. It was originally part of the Lanarkshire and Dumbartonshire Railway line and had two platforms. This line was later taken over by the Caledonian Railway company.

The Beaux Arts design was intended to make the building fit in with other mansions on Great Western Road, then a far cry from the enormously busy traffic route of today. The stations on either side were Crow Road and Maryhill Central, both now shut.

The station was closed during both world wars and was probably regarded as being too remote and open to competition from trams, resulting in its final closure in 1942.

For years, until the line finally closed in 1966, trains still passed through but never stopped, connecting many industrial areas on the north side of the Clyde.

The building itself, comprising a station master's house and ticket office, suffered years of neglect and was the subject of several arson attacks. Happily, it is now a popular restaurant.

NORTH KELVIN MEADOW
AND THE CHILDREN'S WOOD

The last wild space in the West End of Glasgow

Between Clouston Street and Kelbourne Street
Kelvinside, G20 8PR
northkelvinmeadow.com and www.thechildrenswood.co.uk
Buses: 6, 61

Just on the other side of the River Kelvin and the Botanic Gardens, the Children's Wood and North Kelvin Meadow is a very special place. The area used to be playing fields but over time became derelict and scruffy. When developers began to cast covetous eyes on it as a site for new housing, local people put together an effective community group determined to keep the space open for everyone.

Local residents took on Glasgow City Council, who also wanted to develop the area, and it became an epic battle: locals against politicians and property developers, with eviction notices being served on volunteers who had set up bat boxes and raised beds. The volunteers found support among prominent public figures, including Scottish comedian Frankie Boyle, and a protest was held in George Square in 2013. Against all the odds, the campaign to save the Meadow and Children's Wood succeeded in 2016.

Now covered by trees, the former tennis court is now known as the Children's Wood and hosts regular activities for youngsters such as community gardening. Other parts of the meadow contain raised-bed allotments, a wildflower plantation, a fruit garden and a superb orchid site.

Not only does the site offer allotments to local people but it has helped generate a sense of community among many people who have met their neighbours for the first time while volunteering to improve the meadow: yet another sign that community ventures such as this can have a major impact on local life for very little cost.

Julia Donaldson, author of *The Gruffalo*, describes the Children's Wood as 'such a great inner-city open space, a real "secret garden" which serves as an open-air community centre and a place where kids can climb trees and discover nature'. A book has even been published about the struggle to preserve the space. *The Dear Wild Place* by Emily Cutts describes how the Children's Wood was set up and provides information for those thinking about doing something similar within their own communities.

THE SIXTY STEPS

Glasgow's most fascinating external stairway

Between Queen Margaret Road and Kelvinside Terrace, G20 6DA
sixtysteps.org.uk
Buses: 6, 61

The Sixty Steps are the most fascinating external stairway in Glasgow. Connecting Kelvinside Terrace to Queen Margaret Road, they were designed by Alexander 'Greek' Thomson (1817–1875) in the 1870s and their purpose (no longer obvious to the casual passer-by) was to link new housing north of the River Kelvin with a bridge down below. That bridge – the Queen Margaret Bridge – was constructed by a coachbuilder named John Ewing Walker in 1870 but demolished a century later.

If you walk down the steps and look out over the railings across the River Kelvin, you can see at ground level the now obsolete piers upon which the old bridge stood.

When the bridge and the Sixty Steps were constructed in the 1870s, the north bank of the River Kelvin was still open countryside. Walker wanted to encourage new housing to be built in the area, and the bridge was a key part of the plan to allow travellers to come down the Sixty Steps, cross the river and reach the Great Western Road and more populated parts of Glasgow.

At the top of the stairs are superb columns that frame a view over the river down below. They are in the Greek style for which Thomson would become famous although he was also influenced by Egyptian and Indian architectural traditions.

While the Sixty Steps are usually attributed to Thomson, there is surprisingly little documentary evidence from the 1870s to prove that he was the designer. Some people doubt his involvement as he was seriously ill when the steps were built (he died in 1875) and the construction is unlike anything else he attempted. However, this is a minority opinion.

The details of the construction are fascinating. For example, an empty doorway has been cut into the retaining wall ... perhaps signifying Thomson's thoughts on mortality, with the door representing a passageway into the next life.

There are actually sixty-six steps if you care to count as you walk up (or down).

In recent years, the stairs and their massive retaining wall have fallen into disrepair. However, the Greek Thomson Sixty Steps Preservation Trust has been set up to repair and preserve one of Glasgow's most interesting sites for future generations. Readers who are interested in volunteering can find more information on its website: sixtysteps.org.uk/

POETRY POST BOX

The city's quirkiest post box

Glasgow Botanic Gardens, 730 Great Western Road, G12 0UE
Hillhead Subway station

The city's quirkiest and most artistic post box is, without doubt, the striking ceramic example outside the café in the Botanic Gardens. Covered with small creatures, the exterior has a message saying, 'Please post your poems here'.

The Poetry Post Box was installed in 2009 as part of an initiative led by writer and performer Stewart Ennis. At the time, primary school children in Glasgow were encouraged to write and post their poems in the Poetry Box, and since then poems have continued to be posted here and published.

The post box is the work of Julia Smith (b. 1974), a graduate of the Glasgow School of Art who now lives in the Highlands. At the time, she talked of how local primary school children 'visited the Botanics and sketched plants, insects and animals they saw there and then came up with combinations of them and wrote poems about their creations. The creatures can be found hidden amongst the foliage on the Poetry Post Box.'

The first-ever poem posted in 2009 was by a girl named Flora from Hyndland Primary School. Entitled 'Last night in the park I saw', it includes the following lines:

Last night in the park I saw
A crocodile with a wonky jaw
I asked him if he was ok,
He answered, 'yes, now I'm going to a play.'
Last night in the park I saw
A man telling someone about the law,
He said it was great, that he should give it a go.
Only then did I realise he was talking to a Crow.

Nowadays Flora is herself a primary school teacher.

NORTH WOODSIDE FLINT MILL

Ruins of a historic mill

North bank of River Kelvin
Kelvin walkway (reached from Kelvin Drive or Glasgow Botanic Gardens),
G20 6DW
Hillhead Subway station

The River Kelvin begins in the area of Kilsyth and flows around 35 km south, through Glasgow, before emptying into the Clyde. Several water-powered mills used to stand along its banks – the substantial remains of one survivor can still be seen opposite the Botanic Gardens.

The North Woodside Flint Mill was built in 1846; its purpose was to grind down flint for use in the manufacture of crystal glass and pottery. The flint was often imported to Glasgow, sometimes taken from boats that used it as ballast. It was then burnt in a kiln on the site and ground

down using millstones until it formed a creamy paste. This was dried and cut into blocks before being carted away to manufacturers.

The mill was founded to supply the Verreville crystal glass and pottery works in Finnieston. There, the ground flint from the mill helped make crystal glass sparkle and created a particularly hard glaze in pottery production.

This is an especially historic location as there was an even older mill on this site, dating from the mid-18th century. It was initially used to ground barley but later produced gunpowder for the Napoleonic Wars.

Today you can still see the ruins of the lade that channelled the river water used to power the mill. Remains of the kiln, millstones and other parts of the 19th-century buildings are also clearly visible.

Perhaps surprisingly, flint continued to be ground using water power right up the mill's closure in around 1960. The ruins are a rare reminder of a past age when water-powered mills were an important part of the city's economy.

GLASGOW BOTANIC GARDENS LOST STATIONS

Ghostly remains

730 Great Western Road, G12 0UE
Hillhead Subway station

If you head off the main paths, Glasgow's famous Botanic Gardens contain the forgotten and fascinating ghostly relics of two old suburban train stations.

The first is visible if you walk through the main entrance off Great Western Road and bear left. Here – just behind some trees – lie the remains of the Botanic Gardens Railway Station originally operated by the Glasgow Central Railway.

It opened in 1896 and the platforms that are still visible were below ground level. The station continued to be used until 1939 when it was closed, a victim of competition from tramlines and the over-expansion of suburban railway lines. Sadly, the landmark station building up above the platforms was ravaged by a fire in 1970 and later demolished.

The Glasgow Central Railway was built by the Caledonian Railway and ran mostly through tunnels right through central Glasgow. At this time, there was competition between the railway companies to reach the city's expanding suburbs, but construction was hugely expensive and difficult with miles of underground tunnels having to be dug out. Many passengers disliked the experience as standing on underground platforms with a steam train passing through was not always very pleasant! The Glasgow Central Line finally closed in the mid-1960s.

While in the Botanic Gardens, take the opportunity to see the much harder-to-find remains of Kirklee railway station, which used to be just one stop along on the Glasgow Central Line. It also opened in 1896 and closed in 1939. It was designed by Sir John James Burnet, an eminent Scottish architect responsible for Charing Cross Mansions and the Glasgow Savings Bank on Ingram Street. After closure, the station building was used as a private residence before being demolished in 1971.

Most of the site has been built over but if you enter the Botanic Gardens from Ford Road and walk along the path before bearing left through the trees, you will see the platform remains. If you look back along Ford Road, you can see the remains of a railway bridge adjoining the gardens. The platform is behind these remains.

WINDOWS IN THE WEST TENEMENT

Scene of one of the public's favourite paintings

35 Saltoun Street, Dowanhill, G12 9AR
Hillhead Subway station

S tand outside 35 Saltoun Street, not far from Byres Road, and you'd be forgiven for imagining this was just another smart West End tenement. However, it is in fact the subject of *Windows in the West*, the public's best-loved portrayal of a Glasgow scene.

The painting is the work of Avril Paton. On a snowy day in January 1993, she looked out of the window of her flat opposite and was inspired to capture the wintry scene in paint. The work, which took six months to complete, featured Paton and several real residents of No. 35 that she knew, including people at a party, a man working at his computer and someone peering out of a window.

The painting was later hung in the city's Concert Hall and quickly became popular. It is hard to know why some paintings resonate with the public and others do not, but people seemed fascinated by the animated lives of the tenement's residents, which contrasted with the cold Glasgow scene outside. This popularity led to the painting being moved to the Museum of Modern Art and then after several years to its current home – the Kelvingrove Art Gallery.

Over time, the popularity of *Windows in the West* has continued to grow, as evidenced by the fact that prints of the painting are regularly the best-selling items in the Gallery's gift shop. It also fascinates people outside Glasgow, and the film director Danny Boyle specifically chose a print of *Windows in the West* to feature in his film *T2 Trainspotting*. Paton is regularly approached by people wanting to make musicals, films and animations inspired by the painting.

This success was not something Paton could have envisaged back in 1993 when her name was not familiar to the public. Born in Glasgow in 1941, she spent her early years on the Isle of Arran before attending the Glasgow School of Art. She only lasted a year, then got married and had two children. When the marriage failed, she returned to Arran – as a single mother. She lived in a squat for several years, and her first break came when her painting *The Barras* was bought by the Council for the People's Palace. Paton then secured a job as a live-in caretaker with Glasgow West Housing Association at the building opposite No. 35, all the while juggling her job, motherhood and developing her career as an artist.

The painting features a party hosted by a fun-loving resident named Norman (on the left, first floor). Paton later recalled how she struggled to think of a title, for a while considering *Norman's Cocktail Party*, but

Windows in the West won the day. She says that the title refers both to the location of the tenement and to the way people live their lives in the Western Hemisphere.

Some of the residents featured in *Windows in the West* still live here and Paton is in touch with many of them.

TRAM ROSETTES

A reminder of Glasgow's once great tram system

Junction of Byres Road and Ruthven Lane, G12 8UB
Hillhead Subway station

Before it closed down in 1962, Glasgow's tram network was perhaps the most extensive in Europe. If you had walked around the city in 1950, you could hardly have avoided seeing tramlines, tramcars or electric cabling at some point – unsurprising, given that around 1,200 trams crisscrossed the city over 160 km of rails. However, today you have to look hard to see any remains of this once magnificent civic transport system.

One relic is still visible if you walk down Byres Road, stop at the junction with Ruthven Lane and look up at the first floor of the neighbouring building. You will see some old tram 'rosettes' – anchors for the overhead tram wires that provided electricity to the tramcars and their motors. They were called rosettes as their design incorporated floral decorations.

The city's tram system was inaugurated in the 1870s, originally using horse-drawn tramcars. However, the network had been electrified by 1902, and replacing horses with electric motors required an enormous development of infrastructure – from new electricity stations to electric cables tethered to walls all around the city. It also meant that many horses, stables and associated jobs disappeared, never to be replaced.

The tramlines running down Byres Road were part of route 5. The greater use of cars and buses led directly to a decline in demand for the trams and the system began to be phased out from 1956.

On 4 September 1962 the final tram set out on its journey: 250,000 Glaswegians turned out to see it. It marked the end of the last tram system in Britain (aside from Blackpool) and many in the city were very sad to see it go.

In recent years trams have been reintroduced in several British cities, including Edinburgh, but – sadly – not Glasgow.

An original tramcar

If you want to see an original tramcar of the kind that would have been a familiar sight on Byres Road, visit the Riverside Museum in Glasgow or the Summerlee Museum of Scottish Industrial Life in Coatbridge. The latter has a short working tramline and is also restoring an original Glasgow tramcar (see: culturenl.co.uk/summerlee/ or call 01236 638460).

PANELLING AT THE UNIVERSITY CAFÉ

Memories of the city's shipbuilding past

87 Byres Road, G11 5HN
Daily 11am–8pm
Kelvinhall Subway station

Founded in September 1918 by Pasquale Verrecchia, the Scots-Italian University Café on Byres Road has served generations of Glaswegians with fish and chips and ice cream (Jamie Oliver is a fan!). Its vintage interior makes visitors feel like they're stepping back in time, the walls lined with photographs showing members of the Verrecchia family over many years. Take time to look at the wooden panelling on the wall facing the entrance: it's a surprising and little-known link to the city's shipbuilding heyday and the carpentry skills of Pasquale himself.

Pasquale came from Cassino in central Italy, where he trained as a carpenter. Like many thousands of Italians, he fled poverty at home to start a new life in Glasgow. He first worked on a farm and then at a shipyard, at a time when Glasgow's shipbuilding industry was at its peak. He joined some 70,000 other workers who toiled away across 19 shipyards that were then producing many of the largest, most sophisticated ships in the world.

Pasquale's excellent carpentry skills led to him becoming a trusted employee at one yard, producing elaborate but functional interiors for grand liners and warships. But he was ambitious and, like many Italian immigrants, dreamed of opening his own café.

In the late 19th century, Italians began to appear in Glasgow, often selling ice cream on the streets from carts. By the First World War, the Italian community had become more prominent and many within it had progressed from ice-cream carts to running their own cafés. On their way back from the pub at closing time, working-class Glaswegians would stop at Italian-run cafés to line their stomachs with cheap food, while youngsters sat for hours over a soda or an ice cream.

Pasquale's bosses at the shipyard were keen to keep him but in 1918 he fulfilled his dream and opened the University Café. According to Verrecchia family legend, he used wood found at the shipyard to fit out his new business. Pasquale's descendants still run the café today and tell of how he carved the panels in the rear of the café before fitting them on the walls inside. The original panelling seen today is a legacy of the era when Glasgow's shipyards were the envy of the world.

Look out for a photograph inside showing Pasquale and his wife standing proudly outside the café, the windows displaying adverts for Three Castles cigarettes and Capstan Navy Cut.

QUAKER BURIAL GROUND IN PARTICK

Glasgow's smallest and most forgotten graveyard

Keith Street, G11 6QQ
Partick train and Subway station, Kelvinhall Subway station

The once working-class district of Partick has plenty of housing apart from the famous Glasgow tenements, including pockets of mid-20th-century red brick houses and flats that are out of touch with (but also synonymous with) the ever more cosmopolitan area surrounding them. In the middle of one of these tiny housing schemes lies another curiosity: Glasgow's smallest graveyard, tucked away on the corner of Keith Street, away from the hum of traffic on Beith Street and the bustle of Dumbarton Road.

It's a 'blink and you'll miss it' spot: a small patch of grass surrounded by metal railings. There are no gravestones, no eerie signs to let neighbours know that the dead rest easy next door. There is, however, a wooden plaque singling it out as a Quaker burial ground, gifted by John Purdon in 1711 and maintained by the Society of Friends.

Last used in 1857, the Quakers later donated the site to Partick, allowing building to go on around it in exchange for the site being kept in good order. The council (or the residents) seem to be keeping their end of the bargain as the burial ground remains, while the land around it becomes ever more valuable.

John Purdon was a member of a well-known Quaker family and his wife, known as 'Quaker Meg' (no points for originality here), was the first person interred there. The family name lives on in nearby Purdon Street, parallel to Keith Street and the tiny graveyard – another curiosity for anyone with an interest in Partick's history.

Unfortunately, without headstones, the Quaker burial ground holds less appeal than the grandeur of the city-centre Necropolis. As Billy Connolly once said, '[Glasgow] doesn't care much for the living, but it really looks after the dead' – a sentiment that's plain to see in Glasgow's City of the Dead, but less obvious in this western corner, where the Quakers have just a single plaque to commemorate them.

MASONIC LODGE

One of Glasgow's most amazing hidden places

92 Dumbarton Road, G11 6NX
To visit the Masonic Temple: partickstmaryslodge.com
Also open during Glasgow Doors Open Day
Kelvinhall Subway station

On Dumbarton Road, which is full of typical Glaswegian tenement buildings and shops, look up at No. 92. You will see a curious sign containing a compass set with the letter 'G' at the centre, evidence that this building is connected to Freemasonry.

Inside, the atmospheric Masonic Temple on the first floor is one of Glasgow's most amazing hidden places. The temple is richly decorated and brightly coloured, the highlight being the many mysterious symbols of Freemasonry – the all-seeing eye, globes, images of the sun and moon – and the letter 'G' (possibly standing for Great Architect of the Universe).

This whole tenement block, which used to be a dance hall, is owned by Partick St Mary's Masonic Lodge No. 117, one of the oldest Masonic lodges in Glasgow, having been established in 1769. Local lodge members have done a fantastic job gathering memorabilia not just connected to Masonic activities in Partick, but the area's history in general – it is possibly Glasgow's most unique unofficial museum.

When the lodge was founded, Partick was a small village far from the heart of Glasgow. Weathering the Industrial Revolution and the transformation of Partick into a heavily urbanised area within the city, the lodge has been based here since 1908.

Glasgow has 77 individual lodges, all of which are independent of each other but supervised by the Provincial Grand Lodge of Glasgow and part of the Grand Lodge of Scotland based in Edinburgh. There are Scots-founded lodges in every part of the world where Scots have emigrated, so the Freemasons who come to Dumbarton Road are loosely connected to fellow Masons in lodges in Africa, North and South America, and New Zealand.

LION AND UNICORN STAIRCASE

A historic staircase loved by Einstein

University of Glasgow
University Avenue, G12 8QQ
Kelvinbridge Subway station

To the casual visitor, the Lion and Unicorn Staircase at Glasgow University might not stand out amid the glorious neo-Gothic buildings on all sides. The staircase is not large, just a few steps up to a landing before an abrupt twist to the left. There are two other staircases nearby, and every day (during term time) hundreds of students pass by without giving the Lion and Unicorn a second thought. So why, in August 1933, did a visiting Swiss-German professor (Albert Einstein) insist on walking up and down this particular staircase? And why was he so fascinated by it?

By the time Einstein came to Glasgow to accept an honorary degree and deliver a lecture, he was feted around the world and hundreds of other universities wanted to be associated with him. He turned down many offers to visit them, but agreed to come to Glasgow. He held the university in high regard as it had produced many of his heroes: people such as Adam Smith, James Watt and physicist Lord Kelvin who, like Einstein, had changed the world around them forever.

Founded in the mid-15th century near the Cathedral on the east side of the city, the original university then spread out along the High Street. The work of stonemason William Riddel, the staircase was constructed at the original site in 1690. The lion represents England and the unicorn has been the symbol for Scotland since the 12th century. When James VI of Scotland became king of England in 1603, he wanted to promote unity between the countries, so one of the two unicorns then part of the Royal Scottish Arms was dropped in favour of the English lion. The statues on the staircase therefore had a clear political significance for the Glaswegian of three centuries ago.

The university moved to its current site in 1870 and the old buildings by the High Street were then demolished. Only two substantive fragments of the original campus remain: this staircase, and a façade that faces onto University Avenue. Both were carefully moved and rebuilt here.

Another secret

When Einstein walked up and down here in 1933, he was delighted to be treading the same steps as his heroes once had, but he was probably unaware of another secret: originally the staircase turned to the right, but in 1929 this was changed so the second flight turned to the left instead (as you see today).

THREE SQUARES GYRATORY SCULPTURE

A Glasgow connection to Getty

University of Glasgow (West Quadrangle), G12 8QQ
Kelvinbridge Subway station

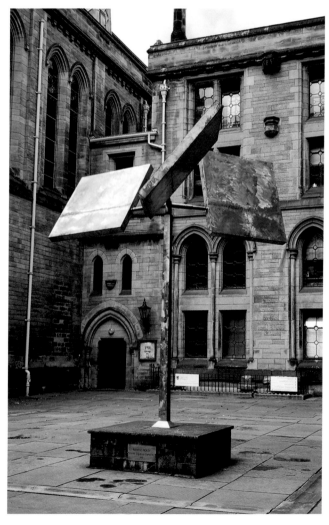

In the centre of Glasgow University, beside the cloisters, is an intriguing and (on a windy day) mesmerising kinetic sculpture entitled *Three Squares Gyratory*. The slightest breeze causes one of the rectangular 'arms' to rotate, although when it's a calm day, it happens so slowly that many passers-by do not realise there is any movement at all.

This shadowy part of the university has a surprising link to sunny California: a very similar piece, also called *Three Squares Gyratory*, is held by the Getty Centre in Los Angeles, part of the prestigious J. Paul Getty Museum.

In shadow much of the day, the sculpture – dating from 1972 – is the work of George Rickey (1907–2002). Born in the United States, he was the son of an engineer and a clockmaker. His parents instilled in him a fascination with engineering and mechanics, something that would inspire his later work as a sculptor. As a child, Rickey lived in Scotland and it is said he learned about the wind and sails while spending time on his dad's boat on the River Clyde.

Rickey's work often featured large kinetic sculptures that involved moving parts. They proved to be very popular around the world with public authorities and other institutions, such as Glasgow University and the Getty, which were looking for artworks to install in public spaces.

In this piece, each of the rectangular 'sails' moves in the slightest wind, but they are designed to be as unpredictable as possible, Rickey wanting to encourage people to stop and watch. Rickey's focus was as much on movement as appearance. He once described his work as 'useless machines'.

BLACKSTONE CHAIR
AT THE HUNTERIAN MUSEUM

Like the Hogwarts Sorting Hat ...

Gilbert Scott Building, University of Glasgow
University Avenue, G12 8QQ
0141 330 4221
gla.ac.uk/hunterian/
Tuesday–Saturday 10am–5pm, Sun 11am–4pm
Free
Hillhead Subway station
4 or 4A First Bus to University Avenue

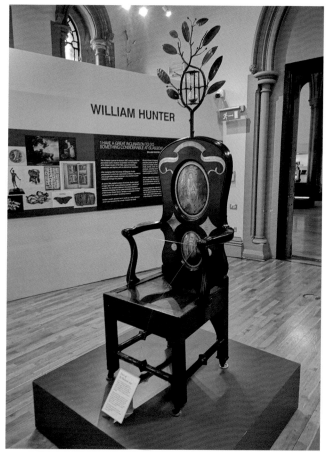

Comparisons between Glasgow University's Gothic spires and the fictional magic academy of Hogwarts, where Harry Potter and his friends study wizardry, have been drawn since J.K. Rowling's books first appeared. It's not hard to imagine Harry and co. playing a round of Quidditch in the university cloisters or brewing up potions in Bute Hall. And so a certain artefact housed in the Hunterian Museum, within the university's Gilbert Scott Building, may also ring a bell with visiting Potterheads.

A slice of history from the university itself, the curious Blackstone Chair takes pride of place when it's not in use for honorary graduations or examinations. Much like the Hogwarts Sorting Hat, the chair (or parts of it) has been used to determine the futures of bright young students since the university was founded in 1451. Back then, students were examined orally, seated upon the Black Stone, a dolerite slab.

In the 18th century, the stone was embedded in an oak chair incorporating the University of Glasgow coat of arms and the names of its founders (Pope Nicholas V, King James II of Scotland and Bishop Turnbull of Glasgow) as well as the Royal Arms of Scotland and England.

The chair today is topped by an ornate bay leaf branch and an hourglass filled with sand, used to count down how long a student has to complete their examination.

With so many students now passing through Glasgow University, it may not be possible to examine them all individually over the Black Stone. But back in 1775, when the chair was made, the bedellus (mace-bearer) would set the timer (which counts around 20 minutes), then shout '*Fluxit!*' ('It has flowed through') to conclude the exam. Not a lot of time, but no doubt a lifetime to some poor students struggling through. If the examiners were satisfied, you passed; if not, the hourglass was reset and you had to do it all over again!

Thankfully, this on-the-spot grilling came to an end for most students during the 19th century. Today, however, the chair is still used for the Cowan Medal, a Mastermind-style competition dating back to 1839 and singling out the best student in his or her year.

BEARSDEN SHARK

See remnants of its last supper in its belly

Hunterian Museum
Gilbert Scott Building, University Avenue, G12 8QQ
0141 330 4221
Tuesday–Saturday 10am–5pm, Sun 11am–4pm
Free
Hillhead Subway station
Buses: 4, 4A

The affluent suburb of Bearsden, just outside the city limit in East Dunbartonshire, seems an unlikely location for the Discovery Channel's Shark Week. For a start, the area is miles from the coast – so the likelihood of running into Jaws and an ominous fin are slim to none. And that's why a trip to the Hunterian Museum is a must: because few people, even those born and raised in Bearsden, know that the area has its very own famous shark.

The Bearsden Shark is 330 million years old and somewhat less toothy nowadays. This unique fossil was discovered in the area in 1982 at the Manse Burn. Fossil hunter Stan Wood is credited with the find, having led the dig and even roped in local schoolchildren to help, although the story goes that he was initially alerted to the site by a local boy who brought him an interesting piece of rock.

The uncovering of a 1-metre-long *Akmonistion zangerli* followed: it's the only complete shark fossil of its kind across the world. And you thought Bearsden was most famous for its golf clubs, good schools and ever-soaring house prices ...

The *Akmonistion zangerli* is extinct, as you would expect, although images of the early carboniferous ratfish are available online, showing a curious shark creature with a dorsal fin in the shape of an anvil or chimney. The Hunterian fossil outlines this perfectly, and more too.

It's a rare example of a cartilage skeleton remaining practically intact when only hard shell or bone usually endures. And the famous Bearsden shark even has remnants of its last supper in its belly: experts say the partially digested remains of a fish can still be seen as well as muscle tissue and blood vessels.

For anyone asking where it came from, the complicated answer lies in shifting land masses. All those millions of years ago, what we know as Scotland was located near the Equator (something many would give their front teeth for on cold, rainy days in present-day Glasgow).

The *Akmonistion zangerli* would have lived in tropical lagoons or swamps created by warm seas, feeding on fish and other sharks. Thick mud on the bottom provided the ideal conditions for preserving our sadly deceased shark, to the delight of paleontologists and modern-day visitors to the Hunterian Museum.

SUFFRAGETTE OAK

Commemorating women winning the right to vote

Kelvin Way, Kelvingrove Park, G12 8QQ
Hillhead or Kelvinbridge Subway station

At the end of the tree-lined Kelvin Way, a road that goes through Kelvingrove Park, the Suffragette Oak stands apart, surrounded by greenery and against the backdrop of one of Glasgow University's oldest buildings, Pearce Lodge.

Planted on 20 April 1918, the tree commemorates women winning the right to vote. It was placed there, in the leafy west end, by Glasgow's suffrage pioneers, the very women who marched the city streets calling for equality of the sexes.

Of course, the 1918 Act only granted the right to vote to women over 30 who met a property qualification, but there is no denying that it was a momentous year, and one no doubt celebrated by the ladies of nearby Queen Margaret College (the University of Glasgow had been accepting female students since 1883).

Today, the Suffragette Oak bears a plaque, installed by Glasgow District Council in 1995, which reads: 'This oak tree was planted by Women's Suffrage Organisations in Glasgow on 20 April 1918 to commemorate the granting of votes to women. This plaque was placed here by the Women's Committee, Glasgow District Council, 8 March 1995.'

Since then, various tributes have appeared by the leafy memorial, including an 'armband' across the trunk in 2018, marking 100 years since it was first installed.

That 100th year followed a spot of bad luck, however. Glasgow's most important tree was damaged during Storm Ophelia in 2017, leaving the City Council no choice but to reduce its height and canopy. Up to 30 per cent of the tree was lost.

Interestingly, the remnants were not discarded. Instead, they were gifted to the Glasgow Women's Library and used to create new items that could be sold on, allowing Glaswegians a chance to own a little slice of local history and furthering the work of another great organisation focused on the education and wellbeing of city women.

Scotland's Tree of the Year in 2015

The Suffragette Oak was named Scotland's Tree of the Year in 2015, marking its beauty and strong, long-standing message to the people of Glasgow.

PEARCE LODGE

Remains of the old university campus

University Avenue, G12 8LU
Kelvinbridge Subway station

In the mid-15th century the University of Glasgow was founded in the east of the city, then just a relatively small settlement that stretched out along the High Street and down to the Clyde. A late 17th-century engraving of the university – known as Old College – shows a large, elegant campus with courtyards and tall towers.

By the mid-19th century, however, the area around the university had changed: it was badly polluted by the nearby large chemical works and surrounded by tenement slums. The university authorities took the momentous decision to move the whole campus right across Glasgow to more salubrious surroundings where buildings suitable for the modern world could be constructed. The site chosen was a few kilometres to the west in Woodlands.

Sadly, the decision to relocate the university resulted in the Old College buildings being demolished in the 1870s. Very little of Old College was saved, but the late 17th-century entrance gate that stood on the High Street was taken down, brick by brick, and then incorporated into the Gilmorehill site. Unfortunately, the old metal studded wooden gate was not brought across as well.

The gateway and gatehouse were named Pearce Lodge after Sir William Pearce, then connected to the famous Fairfield shipbuilding company. A plaque on the gate reads: 'This incorporates the old main gateway and other features from the High Street frontage of the Old College, built in the time of Charles II. It is named after Sir William Pearce, whose generosity made possible its reconstruction on the present site in 1887–88.'

The architect responsible for incorporating the Old College entrance into the new structure was Alexander George Thomson. He had protested at the demolition of the Old College campus, so the creation of Pearce Lodge represented a small victory.

THE 'C' AND 'R' MONOGRAM

The Golden Age of railways

Caledonian Mansions
Caledonian Crescent, G12 8JJ
Kelvinbridge Subway station

The fine red sandstone terrace facing Great Western Road is hardly unusual in Glasgow but walk along the east side, on Caledonian Crescent, and you'll see a stone monogram on the wall displaying the letters 'C' and 'R'. This is a hidden reminder that the sponsor of this construction was the long-defunct Caledonian Railway company, one of Scotland's greatest privately owned railway enterprises.

The Caledonian Railway's origins go back to the mid-1840s, when there was huge investment in the railway infrastructure throughout Britain. The railway revolution of the 19th century had a profound impact on society just as the internet has changed our own era. The railway's directors invested in everything from railway stations, tracks and hotels to locomotives. Thousands were directly employed by the railway companies and many more livelihoods were linked to their success, from coalminers, architects and labourers to lawyers, bankers and metal workers.

The architect James Miller (1860–1947) became a major beneficiary of the Golden Age of the railways. He won so many commissions from the Caledonian Railway that other architects in Glasgow began to resent his success. His prolific career lasted from the late 1880s right up to the early 1940s and he designed dozens of hotels, banks, schools, hospitals, churches and houses, a number of which still exist in Glasgow. However, he is best remembered for his work for the railway.

But why did the Caledonian Railway invest in a mansion block here where there is no railway station? If you walk down the steps to the pathway below the Kelvinbridge, you'll see the bricked-up old entrance to the Kelvinbridge railway station. Opened in 1896, it was operated by the Caledonian Railway but closed to passengers in 1952. After the line was closed to freight traffic in the 1960s, the station building was destroyed by fire in 1968. The next station on the line was at the Botanic Garden (see page 40).

Miller was employed to design both the station and the Caledonian Mansions above, originally meant to be the annex to a grand hotel. The mansions were completed in 1898.

By the early 20th century, it had become clear that the great expansion of the railway companies had gone too far. There were too many to remain profitable, so a wave of consolidation began. The Railways Act led to the Caledonian Railway being absorbed into the London, Midland and Scottish (LMS) Railway in 1923. The great era of investment in railway buildings such as the Caledonian Mansions was coming to an end as cost-cutting took priority.

GARGOYLES AT ST MARY'S EPISCOPAL CATHEDRAL

A cheerful cherub and other strange faces

300 Great Western Road, G4 9JB
Kelvinbridge Subway station

The tall spire of St Mary's Episcopal Cathedral is one of the famous landmarks on the Great Western Road but nearly everyone walks past without noticing the unique gargoyles on the side of the building. Make sure to stop and look closely at the side of the Cathedral facing the street. At first, you may not notice anything but look closer: you will see a line of gargoyles, some of which look a little odd. A few have glasses, one is smiling ... and their faces look suspiciously modern compared to the worn gargoyles on either side.

Historically, gargoyles first appeared on Gothic cathedrals and churches, often used to help drain rainwater away from the building. Masons carved faces that were often grotesque, probably designed to guard the sacred place from evil spirits. Other common designs include saints and holy figures.

In around 2000, however, when St Mary's was nearing the end of a twenty-year renovation scheme, it was decided that many of the people closely involved in the project should be honoured by having their likenesses used for new gargoyles. Around twenty new faces – based on workmen, fundraisers and clergymen – were carved. Two of those immortalised were the Very Rev. Griff Dines, then provost of the Cathedral, and the Right Rev. Idris Jones, Bishop of Glasgow and Galloway. In 2001 the bishop commented, 'The stonemasons have been very generous – I look like a cheerful cherub.'

The Cathedral building was completed in 1893 and designed by Sir Gilbert Scott, the architect responsible for other well-known buildings such as the Midland Hotel at St Pancras Station and the Albert Memorial (both in London) and the University of Glasgow.

BURNBANK BOWLING CLUB

Inner-city Victorian bowling gem

235 Woodlands Road, G3 6NN
Kelvinbridge Subway station

It's easy to walk down Woodlands Road and be blissfully unaware that a 150-year-old sporting institution, the Burnbank Bowling Club, lies behind a set of ornamental gates. The club was founded in 1866, when bowling was hugely popular in Scotland and the nation's players were shaping the rules of the game and producing other innovations that would be adopted by the rest of the world.

Modern lawn bowling probably developed as far back as the 15th or 16th century. It was certainly played by Scottish kings as long ago as the 1400s. With the industrialisation of Glasgow from the late 18th century, the growing middle classes started to become interested in the game, and clubs sprang up in the new suburbs where the wealthier professionals were now living. Burnbank was typical of this groundswell of popularity and used to be much bigger, with members using the club as a social space rather than just a sporting venue.

Today, Burnbank, like many other clubs, has suffered as the average age of players has crept up and youngsters are harder to attract. However, it encourages visitors and new players and if you're passing by when play is on, you're sure to get a warm welcome.

If you go inside the club house, you'll see a fascinating slice of Glasgow's social and sporting history: the walls are lined with photographs of the club's presidents and players going back over a century. It also shows how the players – and by definition, Glaswegians – have changed over this period, with moustaches and beards of varying lengths and sizes making an appearance as fashions came and went.

Scots who have emigrated are credited with helping to spread the game across the world, particularly to the US and Canada; it is now played in over 40 countries. However, Glasgow is arguably the global game's spiritual home with over 200 public bowling greens. Burnbank is just one of these, but its prime location, hidden away from public view behind hedges, makes it a special place.

ACROBATIC EQUIPMENT AT THE ARLINGTON BATHS

One of the world's few remaining trapeze systems in a swimming pool

61 Arlington Street, G3 6DT
0141 332 6021; arlingtonbaths.co.uk
Annual membership fees, or £15 for trial
Weekly Continental swim £10 for non-members
Free guided tours of the baths can be arranged
St George's Cross Subway station

There are several historic bathhouses in Glasgow, but few are as grand, or as varied in their modern offerings, as the Arlington Baths. But the fact that you can fly through the air on one of the world's few remaining trapeze systems may be the biggest draw for athletic types.

Once popular in the early 1900s, there are now only three swimming pools in the whole of the UK with traditional travelling rings and trapeze equipment – all of them in Scotland and two in Glasgow. Like the Western Baths Club in nearby Hillhead and the Drumsheugh Baths

Club in Edinburgh, the Arlington will let you swing out over the pool with a little bit of instruction from lifeguards.

The idea is that you can travel from one side of the baths to the other without hitting the water – if you're strong enough – and it's easy to imagine the intense workout involved. Of course, fellow pool-goers are asked to avoid swimming underneath while you're in flight … just in case your muscles fail you.

Situated in a side street off Woodlands Road, the Arlington was founded in 1870 as a 'welcoming and peaceful sanctuary for citizens of Glasgow, offering a relaxing getaway in the heart of the city'. 'Luxury' is a word that is too often bandied about, but there are few others that could describe the A-listed Victorian leisure centre, which includes a 21-metre-long skylit swimming pool, opulently decorated Turkish suite, saunas, steam room, free-standing slipper baths and hot tubs, and a modern gym.

Architecturally speaking, the building (designed by John Burnett) is a gem worth investigating: classic stone columns and high wooden beams will certainly keep you occupied while swimming your lengths.

Today, the bathhouse is run by members on a not-for-profit basis, making the Glasgow community one of the oldest clubs of its kind in the world.

A skinny swim club every Sunday

On Sunday nights at the Arlington, things turn decidedly *au naturel*. Glasgow Continental is a weekly skinny swim club running from 6pm to 9pm, open to Arlington members and non-members alike. Naturists can use the facilities, as well as a fully stocked relaxation area, without the need for soggy swimwear. There are naked yoga classes too, offering another outlet for nudists who want to expand their horizons.

The Western Baths Club

With only three trapeze systems left in the UK, it's hard to believe that two of them are in Glasgow. Still, the Western Baths Club merits a mention beyond its rare athletic equipment. Established in 1876 in the wake of the Arlington's popularity, this hidden-away gem is just a stone's throw from one of the busiest streets in Glasgow – Byres Road – and yet few people know about it. The private facilities are well worth the price tag for a glimpse of the swimming pool's vaulted ceiling. Or you can take a virtual tour online at thewesternbaths.co.uk/virtual-tour/.

WOODLANDS COMMUNITY GARDEN

An urban garden in the heart of the city

117 West Princes Street, G4 9BY
woodlandscommunity.org.uk
St George's Cross Subway station

It's easy to walk down West Princes Street in Woodlands and imagine it's just another Glasgow road, but look out for the entrance to one of the city's most innovative and impressive new gardens.

In 2009 a local organisation called Garden Revolutions of the West End – set up by artist Nina Wesolowski and architect Hanna Buss – persuaded the Woodlands Development Trust to let them transform a derelict site opposite Queen's Crescent into a community garden.

The site had been left empty after a tenement building collapsed in the 1970s, and the garden (opened in 2010) quickly became a peaceful oasis beloved by locals notwithstanding its proximity to the M8 motorway.

In just a few years, the garden has brought together the local community in such a positive way that common sense would suggest every part of the city should copy its example. Around 45 families, individuals and couples are involved in growing plants and vegetables in raised beds, and a much wider community of around 500 people are involved in the various on-site activities.

Neighbours who had previously never even met now have a place to socialise and make new friends, as well as grow their own food. Recent arrivals to Scotland, including asylum seekers, mix with born-and-bred Glaswegians, help each other discover cultural connections and reduce isolation and tensions. Using the garden has also proved to be particularly important for those under the care of local institutions, including a mental health charity and a day care centre for the elderly. Highlights of the year include harvest festivals, solstice events, concerts and an anniversary party.

Beside the garden is a community building used for workshops, social events and art projects. Volunteers work in the vegetarian café, organise homework nights for local schoolkids and tackle street littering by organising regular clean-ups. The influence of the Woodlands project is growing and those working at the garden are now involved in mentoring other community gardens seeking to provide similar benefits for their own local residents.

THE ARLINGTON BAR

Scotland's holiest relic

130 Woodlands Road, G3 6LF
Saint George's Cross Subway station

A Glasgow pub in the west end seems an unlikely location for a mythical symbol of Scotland's monarchy which is mentioned in the Old Testament ... but go into the Arlington Bar on Woodlands Road and you can decide for yourself. Situated to the right of the bar is a piece of sandstone that is claimed to be the true Stone of Destiny.

The Stone of Destiny has uncertain origins, but traditionally it is claimed to have been used by Jacob as a pillow, as recorded in the Book of Genesis. It may have been brought to Scotland from the Middle East around 1,200 years ago and became known by the Celtic name Lia Fail, or 'Speaking Stone'.

No one knows for certain how the stone became a symbol of Scotland's monarchy, but for centuries it was used at Scone during coronation ceremonies. In 1296, however, an invading English army under Edward I stole the stone and it was later brought to Westminster Abbey. There, in a calculated snub to Scotland and a clear message of where power really lay, the stone was kept under the coronation chair in the Abbey.

The fate of Scotland's stolen Stone of Destiny rankled with many Scots over the years, and on Christmas Day 1950 some students from Glasgow University decided to set matters right by stealing it back from Westminster Abbey. This audacious act of score-settling created a media furore, with roadblocks set up to try and stop the thieves. However, the students evaded all attempts to recover the stone, bringing it back to Glasgow in their Ford Anglia car. They then celebrated their achievement in the Arlington Bar.

There are differing accounts of what happened after the stone's return to Glasgow. The official version of events is that the enormous public interest in the case made the students lose their nerve and they left the stone at Arbroath Abbey for the authorities to recover. Found by the police, it was returned to Westminster Abbey and was used in the coronation of Elizabeth I in 1953. However, it has long been suggested that the patriotic students arranged for a replica of the stone to be made, and it was this fake that made its way back to London.

According to the Arlington Bar, their hunk of sandstone is the real Stone of Destiny, put on display after it was discovered hidden under a seat in the pub. Officially, the Stone of Destiny currently resides in Edinburgh Castle after being returned from London in 1996 ... but for many Glaswegians the Arlington Bar's claim is preferable and much more fun!

CHARING CROSS MANSIONS CLOCK

The architect who inspired the face of Father Time

2–30 St George's Road, Charing Cross, G3 6UJ
Cowcaddens Subway station

Situated by the M8 and on a busy road junction, Charing Cross Mansions are easy to ignore, particularly as most passers-by are eager to escape the heavy traffic. However, the frontage – and especially the clock featuring Father Time – are two of the best examples of late Victorian decorative architecture in the city.

Completed in 1891, the mansions are regarded as one of Glasgow's finest surviving red sandstone tenements. Designed by John James Burnet (1857–1938) in a French Renaissance style, they are located in what was once an elegant, impressive district. Tragically, Charing Cross's appeal was forever damaged when the M8 motorway was built in the

1970s. A large number of buildings were demolished as a result, but the mansions luckily survived.

If you stop outside the building, it's worth spending a few minutes trying to recognise the various symbols on display and consider the secret behind the face of Father Time – the features are believed to have been based on Burnet himself. Thankfully, he never lived to see his doppelganger being forced to look down on the busy modern roads below.

The sculptures around the clock are the work of William Birnie Rhind (1853–1933), a prolific artist whose work can be seen on several buildings in Glasgow. Just below the clock are the Glasgow City Arms, while above are the statues of a male and female representing Commerce and Industry. Lower down are figures representing the four seasons, a reminder of the passing of time. Rhind is believed to have been heavily influenced in his work by Michelangelo.

The Lion of Scotland can just about be seen above the clock face, while the face itself features the signs of the zodiac.

NEARBY
Anderston Library sign
Mitchell Library, G3 7DX
Berkeley Street side
Charing Cross train station

On the north side of the famous Mitchell Library is a doorway above which is a sign for the 'Anderston Library'. However, there is no Anderston Library located here. It is just a ghost sign for a once fine institution that disappeared long ago.

History has not been kind to Anderston. This area of Glasgow was, until 1846, an independent burgh outside the city. It became densely populated but was – literally – torn apart when the M8 motorway was constructed right through its heartland. A population of over 30,000 in 1951 had dropped to less than 10,000 two decades later.

Anderston used to be served by a great library of its own on nearby McIntyre Street. Established in 1904, it was regarded as the finest district library in Glasgow. It was founded by monies bequeathed by the Scots-American industrialist Andrew Carnegie, a legacy that helped establish a number of other public libraries in Glasgow, and many other cities in Britain and beyond. It was this grand library that was demolished to make way for the motorway in 1969. In 1984 a new Anderston Library was set up within the much larger Mitchell Library building. This also closed a few years ago; its collection of books moved into the library next door. All that remains of this local legacy is the ghost sign you see today.

CAMERON MEMORIAL FOUNTAIN ㉞

The 'leaning tower' of Charing Cross

Sauchiehall Street, G3 7UJ
Charing Cross rail station or St George's Cross Subway station
Buses: any bus going to Sauchiehall Street

Pisa may have the monopoly on leaning towers, but Glasgow has its very own, curious local landmark that refuses to stay upright.

Ironically, this leaning fountain on the edge of the busy Charing Cross intersection was built in honour of a man who was teetotal, and presumably never veered off course like the monument which still bears his name.

The Cameron Memorial Fountain stands on the corner of Woodside Crescent and Sauchiehall Street – once the gateway between the city centre and the west end, now sectioned off by the M8 motorway which cuts through Charing Cross. According to the Public Monuments and Sculpture Association, it leans a worrying 10.5 inches (26.67 cm) off to the side.

Tourists might not give it a second glance if it wasn't for the fact that the baroque terracotta fountain, long since dried up, veers off at such an odd angle, as if someone has tunnelled underneath and uprooted it from below. You might even say that the fountain looks a little drunk, like so many locals stumbling past it after a night in the pubs and clubs of Sauchiehall Street.

Built in 1896 by public subscription, it was dedicated to Sir Charles Cameron, newspaper editor of the *North British Daily Mail* (later incorporated into the *Daily Record*) and an MP from 1874 to 1895. Cameron was one of the city's prominent Temperance Movement campaigners. He was responsible for the introduction of the Inebriates Acts, which saw 'habitual drunkards' blacklisted and fines for those who served them alcohol. You have to wonder what Cameron would think of the fountain that commemorates his legacy, 'drunken' stance and all.

To some locals, Glasgow's own 'leaning tower of Pisa' is a landmark in keeping with the city's off-kilter sense of humour. Add in the backstory of the teetotaller so against alcohol and it's another amusing anecdote that you might think could only happen in Glasgow.

It may also stick in the minds of Glaswegians because of the abiding urban legend that the fountain's strange lean is down to the construction of the M8. Still a sore point for many, the motorway that decimated communities on either side of Charing Cross back in the 1960s will be blamed for just about anything.

However, the Cameron Fountain has apparently been tilting off to the side for almost a century. The *West End News* and *Partick Advertiser* reported in 1926 that it 'could fall down' – but almost 100 years later, Glasgow's drunken fountain remains a curiosity on the edge of surely the busiest junction in the city.

RENNIE MACKINTOSH STATUE

The first public statue of Glasgow's leading architect

Argyle Street/St Vincent Street
Anderston, G3 8YJ
Anderston train station

Rennie Mackintosh is one of Glasgow's favourite sons and every year thousands flock to see the buildings he designed. Despite the growing Mackintosh 'trail' around the city, many overlook the fantastic statue of the architect and designer in Anderston.

Unveiled on 10 December 2018 (the 90th anniversary of Mackintosh's death), the statue was created by Andy Scott (best known for *The Kelpies* by Falkirk), perhaps the most influential living sculptor in Scotland today.

Mackintosh was only 60 when he died, his later years unrewarding compared to his early life when his designs changed the face of Glasgow. It seems doubtful that anyone in 1928 would have predicted that the architect would be held in such high regard in the future, or that a statue of him would appear in the city.

The statue was commissioned as part of a long-running regeneration project in Anderston. At the time of the unveiling, Scott said: 'Most of my memories as a Glasgow School of Art student have Mr Mackintosh's beautiful building as a backdrop. His distinctive architectural styling and the sculpted detailing of that building undoubtedly influenced my career path. I am immensely proud to have created this distinctive bronze statue of him, especially here in his home city. There can't be many Scots who deserve recognition more than Charles Rennie Mackintosh.'

The statue is large, weighing in at 3 tonnes and standing 2.8 metres tall. It shows Mackintosh sitting on a high-backed chair of his own design, this particular one based on a chair made for a tea room on Argyle Street in 1898 (one of several 'art' tea rooms he designed for the businesswoman Kate Cranston).

Glaswegians have a tendency to cook a snoot at authority and the Mackintosh statue suffered the same fate as the Duke of Wellington statue in Royal Exchange Square when, just ten days after being unveiled, a traffic cone was placed on the architect's head.

Unveiled by Scotland's First Minister Nicola Sturgeon, it is thought to be the first public sculpture celebrating Mackintosh. Sturgeon said at the time: 'This magnificent new Charles Rennie Mackintosh statue is a fantastic addition to Glasgow and recognizes the incredible legacy of one of Scotland's most iconic architects, designers and artists. It is a privilege to officially unveil Andy Scott's installation, which now stands in pride of place in Anderston ...'

THE BACK GARDEN

A secret garden in Finnieston

19 Brechin Street, Finnieston, G3 7HF
Exhibition Centre train station
*Three open days a year, as well as seasonal events and pot luck 'bring a dish'
days*
*To arrange a visit, contact g3growers@gmail.com or facebook.com/
thebackgardeng3*
Buses: 2, 3, 18

A former fly-tip on a quiet road in Finnieston is an unlikely place for a community garden, but today it is home to an organic fruit and vegetable community garden known as 'The Back Garden'.

Run by the G3 Growers, the site was once used by motor mechanics before becoming a dumping ground. In 2011 a Glasgow-based charity called Annexe Communities obtained money from the Climate Challenge Fund to transform the site into a community garden.

It is a place of quiet seclusion, almost hard to believe given that Argyle Street is just a stone's throw away, although the tall tenement buildings on all sides help protect the site from traffic noise.

The garden has five raised beds, designed to be accessible for disabled members and so that they're far away from old toxins that may still be in the ground due to the site's past usage. Three of the beds work on a crop rotation system while the other two are used for soft fruit and herbs. The garden also has apple, pear, plum, damson and fig trees.

Very little is grown in winter, during which the beds are put to sleep and covered over. In spring, seeds are planted inside the greenhouse and polytunnel. When it's warm enough outside, the seedlings are planted out in the raised beds and plant pots. In summer, everything is in full bloom and is a riot of colour; visitors can spot caterpillars, butterflies, bees and other wildlife.

The garden has around 40 active members. Together they run outreach programmes with voluntary groups, schools, nurseries, local housing associations and businesses.

There are three open days a year, as well as seasonal events and pot luck 'bring a dish' days. All the gardening tasks are shared and the produce is divided among the members.

In recent years, annual produce has reached around 400 kg. The project has now become a focal point for local engagement and raised awareness of the importance of sustainable growing while actively lowering the carbon footprint in the area.

THE HIDDEN LANE

Glasgow's ultimate secret gem

1103 Argyle Street, G3 8ND
thehiddenlaneglasgow.com
Exhibition Centre train station
Buses: X19 or 23/26 from city centre

In trendy Finnieston, the Hidden Lane is one of Glasgow's ultimate secret gems. Blink and you'll miss the entrance: a covered, cobbled alleyway off busy Argyle Street, covered in posters and signs which could be anything between five or fifty years old. Head off the beaten track down this treasure trove of independent shops and businesses and you'll find some of the most creative things going on in Glasgow just now.

The highlight is the Hidden Lane Tearoom: a nostalgic, vintage-style place with mismatched crockery and chairs, as well as one of the best afternoon teas in Glasgow. It's a firm favourite with those who love a bit of retro styling, and there's a private function room used for many a hen or birthday party.

There are far too many other businesses to name, from yoga studios to craft supply shops, jewellers to photography studios – all of them housed in ramshackle, brightly coloured shacks and outhouses. You could be forgiven for thinking you've left hard-nosed Glasgow behind until you hear the accent drifting from one door or another.

It's all topped off by the Hidden Lane Gallery, an exhibition space that since 2009 has been showing work by rising stars on the Glasgow art scene and local legends like Alasdair Gray.

Whether you're in the market for a tarot card reading or a new sideboard from an independent designer, this is the place – and it's a slice of the up-and-coming, ever-creative Glasgow that all visitors should experience.

Some locals will argue that the area now known as Finnieston was always Sandyford and that 'Finnieston' (historically the area near the dock, on the north bank of the river Clyde where the Finnieston crane still stands) is just a construct designed to bump up trendy restaurants and house prices.

THE ARGYLE TREE

A rare tree with healing properties

1231 Argyle Street, G3 8TH
Anderston train station

I f you walk along Argyle Street, you'll see a huge 23-metre-high ash tree towering over the four-storey tenement behind it. Almost opposite the famous Park Bar, the tree looks out of place – there's no other tree approaching its stature anywhere else on the street, or indeed on any other major thoroughfare in the city. People living in the flats behind are blessed by the foliage but also literally live in its shadow.

At least 150 years old, the tree has survived the Blitz, pollution, car accidents and attempts by the authorities to cut it down. It's probably the most special tree in Glasgow, one that began to sprout during the reign of Queen Victoria.

There are various local legends about its origins, but perhaps the most attractive tells of a man who planted some primrose roots here that contained the seeds of this ash tree. Franklin Terrace was built around 1850, so these seeds began to sprout not long after the tenements were constructed.

In the 1980s, a Glaswegian received a shock when he visited his girlfriend in her top-storey flat behind the tree. He brought his dog (which scared the girlfriend's cat) and watched, horrified, as the cat jumped right out of the window. Luckily for him, it landed on the branches of the ash tree and survived.

Apart being lucky for cats, the Argyle Tree has mystical significance as the ash, particularly in Norse mythology, has long been regarded as the Tree of Life and is believed to have healing properties.

An ash has a life expectancy of around two hundred years, so this landmark on Argyle Street may not be around for ever. Across Europe, many ash trees have disappeared due the scourge of a fungal disease called ash dieback, but this Finnieston landmark has so far managed to escape the threat.

Another old ash tree

The city's oldest ash is found at the Botanic Gardens. Planted first in the original Botanic Gardens near Sauchiehall Street in 1818, this weeping ash has been located here since 1841.

FORMER MASONIC BUILDING

Mysterious Masonic symbols

8–10 Haugh Rd, G3 8TR
Buses: 2, 3

Today this striking red sandstone building in Finnieston is home to the Baitur Rahman Mosque Glasgow. However, if you look closely outside the building, there are a few tantalizing clues as to its original purpose. The first is on either side of a window where the stonework incorporates symbols used by Freemasons in their meeting places, or Lodges.

At the top left, you can see the Square and Compasses. This is unusual as normally both points of the compass are shown as being over the square (in this case, one lies below, the other on top). The Square and Compasses generally represent the Master of the Lodge. On the

opposite corner is the Level, which is the 'jewel' of the Senior Warden, who, along with the Junior Warden, make up the three principal Office Bearers of any Lodge.

At the bottom corners are what appear to be interlacing Cornucopias (or Horns of Plenty), symbolising abundance and nourishment. This is generally attributed to the Lodge Steward, whose duty it is to look after the Brethren and visitors when the Lodge is 'at refreshment'.

At the top are two monster-type characters with open mouths. They may represent gargoyles which were frequently used by medieval stonemasons when constructing churches and buildings. They are generally defined as waterspouts projecting from the upper part of a building or a roof gutter to throw water clear of walls or foundations. Perhaps the stonemason who carved this particular piece was making a statement about his roots? It was medieval stonemasons who formed the first Lodges that would go on to form the basis of the Masonic community in Scotland.

Interpreting Masonic symbols is not an exact science and even among Freemasons their meaning is open to personal interpretation. However, Freemasons frequently use the symbolism of working tools in their ritual and teachings, and in the past were more open about placing symbols like these on their Lodge buildings.

There are two further clues as to the secret history of this building. One stone states, 'Memorial Stone laid by Bro John Graham JP of Broadstone, Provincial Grand Master of Glasgow City 4th June 1904'. Another refers to 'St Vincent Sandyford Masonic Lodge No. 553'.

St Vincent Sandymount Masonic Lodge No. 533 was founded in 1874 and was just one of dozens in Glasgow that built their own meeting places in the 19th and early 20th centuries. This building was completed in 1905, while John Graham was serving as the Provincial Grand Master of Glasgow. Graham was very much a man of the city's Establishment, serving as a Justice of the Peace, Treasurer and Trustee of the Clyde Navigation Trust, and President of the Council of the Institute of Actuaries and Accountants of Scotland.

The Freemasons moved out of this building long ago but St Vincent Sandyford Masonic Lodge No. 533 is still active and is based not far from here at the Masonic Hall, 9 Ardery Street in Partick.

CLYDESIDE DISTILLERY

A fascinating gem

A fascinating gem
100 Stobcross Road, G3 8QQ
0141 212 1401
theclydeside.com
Every day, 10am–5pm
One-hour tours start at £15 per person
Exhibition Centre train station; Partick train, bus or Subway station

Whisky tourism brings visitors to Scotland every year, but how many of them would think to stop in Glasgow for a dram straight from the source?

The Clydeside Distillery may be in its infancy, but it is a fascinating gem at the heart of the ongoing River Clyde regeneration bid, bringing 'liquid gold' back to Glasgow and to the very site where it was once shipped off to the rest of the world.

Built in 1877, the Pumphouse once formed the entry to Glasgow Queen's Dock, from which ships would export whisky to a global audience. The Pumphouse is one of the few remaining remnants of the once-busy port. Interestingly, it was filled in using rubble from nearby St Enoch station, which was demolished in 1977.

The distinctive building may attract interest from the nearby Clydeside Expressway, but for years it lay relatively unoccupied and uninteresting, visited by the odd 'curry karaoke' customer when a restaurant occupied a section, but never truly appreciated as a Glasgow landmark.

News, then, that it would become the city's first central whisky distillery in decades was met with enthusiasm and just a little bit of cynicism – the drink being something of a national treasure, purists wondered how Glasgow could compete with the subtle Speysides or peaty Islay malts.

The Clydeside Distillery opened in 2017, having launched its first distillation in November that year, and the first batch was ready in 2020. But visitors receive more than just samples of the national drink, as the centre acts as both a distillery and a historic visitor centre, showing Glasgow natives and newbies alike how important the River Clyde was to whisky production and to the city as a whole.

The centrepiece of the tour has to be two copper stills, each weighing around 2 tonnes, perfectly placed in a glass-fronted room looking out along the river towards the Riverside Museum (a more established, prized Glasgow attraction) and beyond.

The views from the still house out over the re-burgeoning Clyde really are spectacular, and worth the ticket price alone to see perhaps the most up-and-coming attraction in Glasgow.

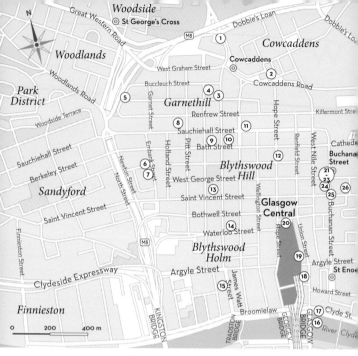

Glasgow Centre

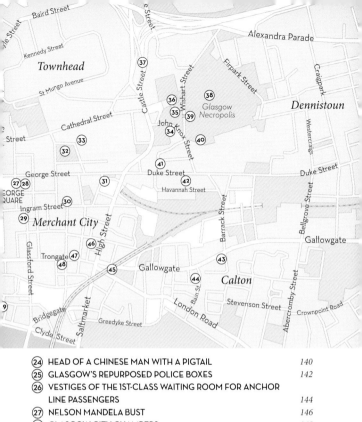

SHADOWGRAPHY IN COWCADDENS

Glasgow's only public example of ombromanie

Cowcaddens Subway station underpass, G4 0SN

The underpass by Cowcaddens Subway station is a pretty grim place, not one that tends to attract visitors. However, a recent piece of street art that adorns its walls deserves some attention. On both sides of the passageway are hands – and a rabbit – depicted as making shadow images against the walls. The work was the result of a collaboration between the artpistol Gallery and the prolific Glasgow aerosol artist Rogue One. The animals emerging out of the shadows include a wolf, a stag, a bird and a cow.

The creation of murals on public buildings to provide an alternative to graffiti and brighten up dingy parts of the city emerged out of the 'Clean Glasgow' initiative in 2008, and now the mural trail can be followed to

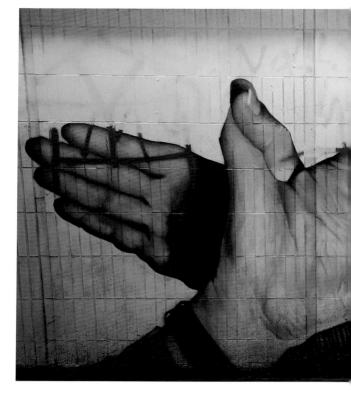

see some of the better-known works. This example of shadowgraphy (or ombromanie as it is also known) is perhaps the most unusual and most hidden example, and you only become aware of the huge hands once you have begun to walk through the dimly lit subway.

The artpistol Gallery has carried out several projects with local graffiti artists to transform previously neglected urban spaces like this, and it has forever changed how parts of central Glasgow are perceived by locals and visitors alike.

The artpistol has also played an important role in the last few years by encouraging young artists who might otherwise have remained obscure, allowing them to earn some money by selling their work commercially.

Rogue One – real name, Bobby McNamara – is a veteran on the city's graffiti art scene. When producing the work, he asked people he knew, including his dad, if he could model their hands for shadow puppets. The result is the most unusual underpass in Glasgow, and arguably the whole of Scotland.

Historic bagpipes in a former church

The National Piping Centre
30–34 McPhater Street, G4 0HW
Cowcaddens Subway station
Monday–Thursday 9am-7pm, Friday 9am–5pm, Saturday 9am–noon (closed Sunday)
Admission charges

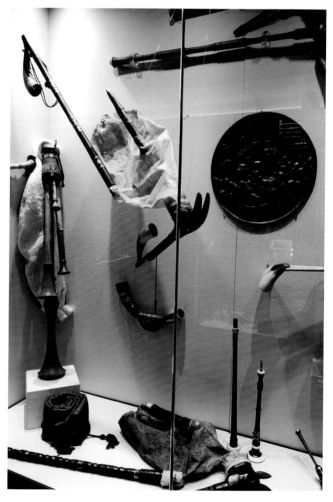

The Museum of Piping is part of the National Piping Centre just north of Cowcaddens Road, which promotes the study of the music and history of the Highland bagpipe. Its patron is Prince Charles.

This small but fascinating museum contains much of the National Museum of Scotland's collection of piping artefacts and its reference library, as well as historical information on the bagpipe going back some three hundred years.

One set on display, from Lochaweside in Argyll, is thought to date from the 18th century. Described as the most authoritative display of its kind anywhere in the world, the museum also contains the Iain Dall MacKay Chanter, a piping relic that belonged to Robert Burns and is the oldest piece of bagpipe in the world. Another highlight is the pipes of John MacColl (1860–1943), one of the most famous of all Scottish pipers.

As well as celebrating the Great Highland Bagpipe, the museum also contains small pipes from the Northumbrian tradition and examples of Polish, Hungarian, Spanish and Italian bagpipes.

Another interesting feature is that visitors can try and play the bagpipes for themselves: no easy task for a novice.

Aside from the museum, the Centre offers bagpipe lessons, workshops and even Gaelic lessons (both here and at a sister site in the West End on Otago Street).

The museum is housed in a superb building dating from 1872, originally Old Cowcaddens Church. Built in an Italianate (Tuscan) style, it is one of the most elegant museum sites in the city.

The building also has its own eight-bedroom boutique hotel and restaurant.

GLASWEGIAN BLACK MADONNA ③

A reminder of Spain's greatest religious relic

St Aloysius' Church
Rose Street, Garnethill, G3 6RE
8am–6.30pm
Cowcaddens Subway station

The exterior of St Aloysius' Church in Garnethill is not the most inspiring in the city, but step inside and you seem to have been transported to a Baroque-era church in Rome. Dating from 1910, the church was built for the Jesuits by a Belgian architect named Charles Jean Ménart, who based his design on St Aubin's Cathedral in his homeland. But it is not the church's Belgian connection that is its most intriguing aspect.

On the right of the altar, inside the Lady Chapel, is a dramatic small statue of the Virgin Mary and Baby Jesus, both wearing gold-coloured clothes, their faces unusually dark. This colouring is a feature of Black Madonnas, a term used to describe similar statues found in other places throughout Europe, most dating from medieval times (see facing page).

This statue is a rare copy of the famous Black Madonna found at the Santa María de Montserrat monastery in Catalonia (see *Secret Barcelona* from the same publisher). The Spanish original has been at the monastery for centuries and is one of the country's most venerated religious images, associated with many miracles and myths.

But why does Glasgow have a copy of one of Spain's Black Madonnas?

In 1522 a troubled young Spanish soldier held an all-night vigil in front of the Montserrat Black Madonna and in the morning he donned the clothes of a beggar. He would later found the Jesuit movement and become venerated as St Ignatius of Loyola. In 2008 representatives of Barcelona football club brought a copy of the Black Madonna to Glasgow when they came to play Celtic. It was appropriately donated to St Aloysius' Church, which is connected to the Jesuits to this day.

Black Virgins: vestiges of pre-Christian religions?

The Black Virgins are effigies of the Virgin Mary (sculptures, icons, paintings) which, for the most part, were created between the eleventh and fourteenth centuries. Their name refers quite simply to their dark colour. Around 500 of them have been counted, mainly around the Mediterranean basin. Usually found in churches, some of them have been the object of major pilgrimages. According to the Roman Catholic Church, there is no theological basis for the colour of these Virgins, although some experts have pointed to the passage in the Song of Songs (1:5): "*Nigra sum sed formosa*" which can be translated as "I am black but beautiful".

Some other very simple reasons have been proposed to explain this black colouring: the colour of the material used (ebony, mahogany, or a dark local wood) or deposits of soot from votive candles. But the importance that this colour has taken over time (some images have even been repainted black during restorations) leads to the belief that a deeper force is at work.

Thus, for some, the colour of the Black Virgin is a reminder that the Virgin, like the Catholic religion in general, did not become established *ex nihilo*, but replaced other ancient faiths in Western Europe: the Mithraic cult (for more details on this fascinating cult which was fundamental in creating a European identity, see *Secret Rome* in this series of guides), Mother-goddess cults, the cult of the Egyptian goddess Isis bearing Horus in her arms, etc. In these archaic contexts, tribute was often rendered to the Mother goddess, symbol of fertility, gestation, procreation, regeneration, and renewal of life in general, on which the peasantry relied to ensure a bountiful harvest.

As the Christian religion began to affirm itself, the Virgin, mother of Jesus, son of God the Creator, thus became associated with this Mother goddess.

In symbolic terms, the black colour of the Virgin naturally evokes that of the virgin earth as well as the maternal/regenerative side of life in the sense that feminine procreation takes place in the (dark/black) depths of the woman's uterus. And her dark colour may also have brought her closer to the peasants whose own skin darkened from working out in the fields in the sun. So it is therefore no accident if similar inscriptions are found on certain statues of Isis as on many of the Black Virgins: "*Virgini paritura*" (to the Virgin who will give birth). Finally, although many of the Black Virgins are associated with miracles, it is interesting to note that these events are usually linked to the beginning of a new cycle or a new era, thus respecting the image of the Virgin as the giver of life, above all else.

GARNETHILL URBAN PARK AND MOSAIC MURAL

Historic public mural and park opened by Princess Diana

Entrance off Hill Street, G3 6RN
Cowcaddens Subway station

A faded mural on a wall overlooking Garnethill Park is a reminder of the regeneration of this area, starting in the 1970s. It is also historic – the predecessor of the murals that have transformed many Glasgow buildings in recent years and become a significant tourist attraction.

This part of Garnethill is just a few blocks south of the thundering M8. In the 1970s Garnethill was very run down, not helped by the bulldozing of large areas to make way for the motorway. However, an exhibition about Garnethill in 1976 at the Third Eye Centre (now the CCA) kickstarted efforts by artists to help transform the area.

The Garnethill Mosaic Mural was one result involving artists and local people. The mural features images that recall Garnethill's history and much of the work was overseen by artist and Garnethill local, John Kraska (b. 1948). The mural incorporates over 180,000 pieces of tiles and is 13 metres wide.

The mural was completed in 1979; many local kids, artists and volunteers helped in its construction. As another indication of how this area has changed over the years, the mural was placed on the wall of a cardboard box factory that has long since closed, as have many other manufacturers and factories that used to be found in Garnethill.

A park and football pitch were part of the original regeneration scheme. However, they were replaced in the early 1990s by the creation of a new urban park that coincided with Glasgow's status as European City of Culture. Much of the credit for the park goes to Germany as the Goethe Institute in Glasgow was involved in the plans and the park was designed by the German environmental artist, Dieter Magnus. It became a template for other urban parks built in Glasgow over later decades.

In 2005 the artist Ulrike Enslein introduced granite slabs bearing quotes from local residents about growing up in Garnethill – try and find these when you visit as they're often overlooked. Also look out for the waterfalls and a memorial stone that records the visit of Diana, Princess of Wales, in December 1991, the year the park officially opened.

GARNETHILL VIEWPOINT

Panoramic view to the west

148 Hill St, G3 6UA
Charing Cross train station or St George's Cross Subway station
Buses: 17, 18, 4, 4A, 6, X25A

There are not many places in central Glasgow with a good view across large swathes of the city and the hills beyond. One of the best is hidden away on the west side on Hill Street in Garnethill. This part of the city was once full of tenements, but many were cleared to make way for the M8 motorway that – sadly – is hard to ignore down below.

One of the few advantages of the clearance of the old buildings was to allow the creation of this viewpoint: a sign lists all the notable landmarks to the south-west and the north.

The pavement has multilingual welcome messages and poems by local people about why they love the viewpoint. The poem by Amaal Kebabti includes the lines:

I see the sunset
I hear the birds chirping in their nests
I taste the natural air
I smell the night sky
I feel the stars
Standing at Garnethill viewpoint

Though it's hard to imagine, just a few decades ago Hill Street ran right on westwards, ending on the other side of where the motorway runs today. The construction of the M8 created a great scar across the city; however, recent planning proposals could see the motorway covered over with a park or other features. If they're approved, this would be a great place to observe how the city changes in the future.

An intimate encounter directly below the viewpoint

The site features in a scene from the film *Wild Rose* (2018), the story of a young Glaswegian woman who leaves prison and wants to further her career as a country and western singer. Rose-Lynn, played by Jessie Buckley, has an intimate encounter with a man directly below the viewpoint.

Echoes of two maritime tragedies

39 Elmbank Terrace, G2 4PT
0141 248 4567
reception@scottishopera.org.uk
Charing Cross train station

Scottish Opera's administrative headquarters on Elmbank Terrace are not generally open to the public. However, if you contact reception during the week, they will normally let you see some of the highlights of this impressive building, notable for its richly decorated interior, marble staircases and stunning series of stained-glass windows.

It's easy to pass by the most unusual feature without noticing it: located near the reception area on the ground floor, a memorial tablet commemorates Scottish engineers who were among the 1,503 people who died when the *Titanic* sank to the bottom of the Atlantic Ocean in 1912. The *Titanic* had no obvious connection with Glasgow, the ship

being constructed at Harland & Wolff in Belfast, so why is the memorial here, in the headquarters of Scottish Opera?

The answer lies in the history of the building, which was commissioned by the Institution of Engineers and Shipbuilders in Scotland. Its grandeur is a reflection of the importance of engineering and shipbuilding to Scotland, particularly to heavily industrialised Glasgow. The nation also produced large numbers of engineers who served on ships in the British merchant navy – at that time, the largest in the world.

When the memorial was unveiled in 1914 it was probably difficult for members of the Institution to imagine that things would ever be different. By the outbreak of the Second World War, a third of all the world's merchant ships were still under British control. In the second half of the 20th century, however, things started to change: the British Empire was dismantled and Glasgow's shipbuilding industry went into a near-terminal decline. Today it is Greece that controls the largest single share of the world's merchant fleet and you are more likely to find an Indian or Chinese engineer on a cargo ship than one from Scotland.

In a sign of the times, the Institute moved out of this grand building in 1968, unable to afford the maintenance costs or make best use of such a large space designed for a different era.

If you walk up the impressive marble staircase, you will find other treasures rarely seen by the public.

On the first floor is Rankine Hall, named after the Institute's first president. A stained-glass window celebrates progress in the fields of engineering and shipbuilding. The central section features another ocean liner that suffered a tragic end.

The *Lusitania* was built at John Brown's shipyard at Clydebank and was for a while the world's largest ocean-going liner. It was sunk after being attacked by a German U-boat in 1915, resulting in the loss of 1,198 lives. Many Americans died in the tragedy and this caused such outrage that it helped bring the US into the First World War on the side of Britain and France, and so changed the course of world history. During the heyday of the grand ocean liners in the early 20th century, the White Star Line (owners of the *Titanic*) and Cunard (owners of the *Lusitania*) were bitter rivals. However, economic pressures during the Great Depression of the 1930s saw the two firms merge to form the Cunard-White Star Line.

On either side of the *Lusitania* are stained-glass images of the *Comet*, an early steamship, and *Rocket*, the first pioneering steam locomotive. They represent just some of the engineering advances celebrated in the Institute's Hall of Fame, which includes such illustrious Scots as James Watt, Thomas Telford, Robert Napier, Alexander Graham Bell and John Logie Baird. While the Institute moved out more than fifty years ago, it still owns the *Titanic* memorial and the stained glass.

THE ELF SCULPTURE

A Welsh elf in Glasgow

Glasgow Botanic Gardens, Kibble Palace, G12 0UE
Daily 10am–6pm
Hillhead Subway station

One of the main attractions at Glasgow Botanic Gardens is the 19th-century Kibble Palace glasshouse. Dotted among its many plants are a number of fine sculptures, one of which is a curious, crouching figure known as *The Elf* (a supernatural humanlike creature in fairy tales, the elf personifies the 'spirits of the air' element in the shamanic tradition), which has strong connections with Wales as well as London.

The statue is the work of a prolific Welsh artist named Sir William Goscombe John RA (1860–1952). As a young man, Goscombe studied in Paris with Auguste Rodin and, as his career developed, won many commissions, particularly in Wales. In this early period his sculptures were known for their naturalistic representation of the human body and *The Elf* was typical of his efforts.

Why an elf? Goscombe grew up in Wales, where elves were part of the folklore. In a book called *British Goblins*, published in 1880, the fairies of Wales were described as coming in five varieties: Ellyllon (elves), Coblynau (mine fairies), Bwbachod (household fairies), Gwragedd Annwn (underwater fairies) and Gwyllion (mountain fairies). Fairies and other folklore tales and myths were particularly popular in the late Victorian and Edwardian periods.

Goscombe exhibited the original plaster version of *The Elf* in 1898 at London's Royal Academy, where the original bronze version is located today. He regarded the statue as his best work and it features in a number of oil paintings made of the artist as well as on the base of his 1942 bronze *Self-Portrait*.

In later years, Goscombe's sculptures became much more serious: war memorials after the First World War and statues of politicians, generals and other notable figures. However, it was the mischievous *Elf*, possibly inspired by stories he heard as a boy growing up in Wales, that was closest to his heart.

The version in Glasgow is a copy of the bronze original that was displayed at the Glasgow International Exhibition of 1901 and purchased by the city council.

The Elf *in Wales*

Glaswegians who have passed by *The Elf* for years may be unaware that a bronze version stands in the castle gardens at St Fagans National Museum of History, near Cardiff. There's also a tiny red wax maquette in Amgueddfa Cymru – National Museum Wales collections at Cathays Park in Cardiff.

A hidden villa within a Greek gem

350 Sauchiehall Street, G2 3JD
Cowcaddens or Buchanan Street Subway station

The Centre for Contemporary Arts (CCA) has long occupied a central place in the city's art scene, hosting everything from film festivals and art exhibitions to Gaelic cultural activities. But if you're sipping a cappuccino in the café on the ground floor, take a moment to look up at the columns and facade of the inner entrance: it's all that's left of an early 19th-century villa that once stood on the hill here.

In 1872 the Building News referred to how 'Sauchiehall-street has, in the memory of those still comparatively young, passed from being a quiet country road to be a busy thoroughfare, so that where but a few years ago the suburban villa was seen nestling snugly among shrubbery and trees, with green lawn and flower plots interspersed, are now to be seen long continuous ranges of tall buildings.' What you see is one of those original villas, built when this part of the city was semi-rural in nature.

So why is it still here? The answer lies with arguably the greatest architect produced by Glasgow – Alexander 'Greek' Thomson (1817–75). Famous for his designs inspired by Greece, Egypt and other ancient civilisations, Thomson was commissioned to build commercial premises here. Completed in 1868, they became known as the Grecian Chambers and as a result the CCA is on the list of sites visited by many 'Greek' Thomson fans.

However, Thomson did not completely demolish the original villa he found on the site and it was incorporated into his design. In 2001, when the CCA was refurbishing the building, the architects rediscovered the remnants of the villa and decided to make it a key feature of the remodelled interior.

In fact, what you see is the old villa on stilts as Thomson excavated under the original building up on the hill and built underneath it. While the Grecian Chambers are the main architectural feature of the CCA building, the old villa's remains are a fascinating reminder of how Sauchiehall Street once looked before being swallowed up by the city's relentless expansion westwards.

MACKINTOSH FRIEZE
AT THE GLASGOW ART CLUB

Mackintosh's lost masterpiece restored

185 Bath Street, G2 4HU
glasgowartclub.co.uk
Guided tours: Tuesday 11.30 am (March–May, October–mid-December). Book through eventbrite.co.uk or call ahead (0141 248 5210)
Charing Cross train station or Buchanan Street Subway station

Surprisingly few people who are interested in Charles Rennie Mackintosh visit the Glasgow Art Club to see a frieze based on one of his original designs. The story of the frieze reads like something from an artistic detective novel.

When he designed it in 1893, the 25-year-old Mackintosh was working as a draughtsman for the architects Honeyman and Keppie. John Keppie was in charge of the project to create a clubhouse for the prestigious Glasgow Art Club. However, he was aware of young Mackintosh's talent (they would later become partners) and shared the design work with him.

Architectural historians still argue over the respective contributions of Keppie and Mackintosh to the design of the club. It seems likely that Mackintosh was responsible for much of the original interior and furnishings, including a horizontal decorative band (or frieze) that ran along the upper wall of the gallery. At the time, the *Evening Times* described the frieze as a 'wall-painting ... all in quiet tones, creams and delicate greens predominating'.

Sadly Mackintosh's frieze disappeared some years later, damaged by leaking water, and was plastered over. A few years ago, the club was being refurbished and it was decided to try and re-create the frieze based on what scant evidence remained under the plasterwork and other sources. The artist Chris Allan, working with Historic Scotland, was primarily responsible for what you can see today. He studied Mackintosh's original sketchbooks closely together with some drawings for the club printed in the *Bailie* magazine in 1893.

The new frieze, an important reminder of Mackintosh's early work, was unveiled to the public in 2014 and is as faithful to the original design as possible.

'CHOOKIE BURDIES'

Unique lamppost birds

Rose Street, Garnethill, G3 6RB
Cowcaddens Subway station

If you wander around Garnethill, remember to look up at the lampposts, perhaps the most unusual you will ever see. Regardless of the weather and wind conditions, staring down at you will always be at least 300 birds. How can you be sure? Because sculptures of a pair of birds – the 'Chookie Burdies' – were installed on 150 lampposts in 1993 as part of a lighting improvement scheme. To have a public artwork so spread out over multiple locations is unprecedented. There is nothing else like it in Glasgow, or indeed in Scotland.

In the early 1990s, the Glasgow Development Agency and Strathclyde Regional Council commissioned East-Kilbride-based artist Shona Kinloch to add something of interest to new lampposts being located in Garnethill. Kinloch based her sculptures on pigeons as she regards them as the true city birds – appropriate given Garnethill's central location in Glasgow. In the following years, she has produced more sculptures inspired by pigeons.

Born in 1962, Kinloch studied art at the Glasgow School of Art in Garnethill, so she knew the area well. She explains: 'The reason for the Chookie Burdies was simply that birds sit on lampposts, so they were the logical conclusion. And even though there are only two different birds, by positioning each bird individually, every lamppost was a one-off which doesn't usually happen with lampposts. I doubt that anyone looking at them would realise unless it was pointed out. I've always liked seeing [real] birds sitting on lampposts and I especially like to see a real bird landing on one of the Chookie Burdies.'

But what are chookie burdies? In Scots, it can mean a small bird or chicken and they feature in a traditional children's rhyme:

Wee chookie burdie toll loll loll
Laid a wee eggy on the windae sill
The windae sill began tae crack
Wee chookie burdie, roared and grat.

When she was a child, Kinloch's mother used to sing the song to her and sometimes called her daughter a 'chookie'. Years later, the sculptor cannot think of her Chookie Burdies without thinking of the rhyme.

According to a Scots-language dictionary, 'chookie burdie' has another meaning: an attractive young woman (*'Before ye ken it, they laddies'll be gettin oaf wi wee chookie burdies at the dancing'*).

JAMES THOMSON'S FACE

The immortal architect

Cambridge Buildings, 202–212 Sauchiehall Street, G2 3EF
Buchanan Street Subway station

Sauchiehall Street is typically so busy that stopping to observe small architectural details on its buildings is usually the last thing on the minds of Glaswegians. However, if you stand at the junction of Sauchiehall Street and Cambridge Street and look up to the third floor, you will see the sculpture of a male face staring out at you.

This is the face of James Thomson (1835–1905), a respected architect in Victorian Glasgow. He would go on to work with his architect sons, James Baird Thomson and William Aitken Thomson. The family architectural practice also employed James Charles Young to provide sculptures and other embellishments for the buildings they designed.

The practice used Young to make small portraits of James Thomson that were added to a few of their buildings. The portraits were not large enough to impact the overall design but clear enough to make a statement about this being a Thomson building.

James Thomson was never a famous architect and few Glaswegians today will have heard of him, but unlike Alexander 'Greek' Thomson or Charles Rennie Mackintosh, James Thomson's face will gaze out over Glasgow for as long as his family's buildings stand.

The two Thomson boys were keen on publicly honouring their father (and boss). However, what clients thought of their architects putting up these sculptures is not known. In the 21st century, it would be seen as incredibly egotistical for any architect to expect to have an image of their face put on one of their buildings. Nevertheless, Thomson's face certainly adds a little charm and a twist to an otherwise nondescript building. Perhaps this was a homage by the two boys to their ageing father.

The building was finished in 1902 and James Thomson died three years later. His sons carried on the family architectural practice for several more years. All three were reunited in death within the Thomson family tomb in Glasgow's Necropolis.

Similar carved portraits of James Thomson were included on the frontage of other buildings designed by the Thomson family in Renfield Street, West George Street and Hope Street.

FORMER MASONIC TEMPLE

Masonic symbols

98–104 West Regent Street, G2 2QD
Glasgow Queen Street train station
Buses: 3, 4, 9, 10

W hile several buildings on West Regent Street display Masonic symbols, the exterior of the former Masonic Temple at No. 98-104 has the most notable examples.

If you look up to the top of the building, you can see a large sun motif with a face at the centre. The sun, moon and stars are commonly-used Masonic symbols, and have been described as referring to God whom the star, moon and stars obey. A sun and moon may also be used to inform members of a lodge to run their business regularly. In the Scottish Rite – a sort of 'rule book' as to how members of Masonic lodges in Glasgow can move through different levels (or 'degrees') of experience – the 28th degree is 'knight of the sun'.

The building, which dates from the mid-1890s, was designed by the Freemason architect James Linburn Cowan. He was commissioned by the Masonic Halls Company to create a grand Masonic Temple that could be used by members of the many lodges established in the city. No expense was spared in the construction of the temple: it had a hall that could accommodate 400 Freemasons, and the interior, exterior and stained-glass windows were covered in Masonic symbols.

The statues of John the Baptist (on the left) and John the Evangelist represent two important figures in Freemasonry. It has been suggested that early Freemasonry drew on pagan traditions and given that the feast day of John the Baptist is 24 June, and that of John the Evangelist is 27 December, this may be linked to the pagan festivals that mark the summer and winter solstices. When placed together, they represent the balance of darkness and light, winter and summer, and life and death.

ROYAL COLLEGE OF PHYSICIANS AND SURGEONS

A medical treasure in the heart of the city

232–242 St Vincent Street, G2
Guided tours by appointment: 0141 221 6072
library@rcpsg.ac.uk
heritage.rcpsg.ac.uk/exhibitions
Library, Library Reading Room and exhibition space open to the public:
Monday 2–5pm (except public holidays)
Cowcaddens Subway station

Although not generally open to the public, you can see many of the Royal College of Physicians and Surgeons' treasures every Monday between 2 and 5pm, and even more of the building if you take a guided tour (contact the College beforehand). The tours allow you to experience a fascinating range of exhibits, from Joseph Lister's graduation gown to original portraits of James I and Princess Diana (a College patron). Not only will you learn about the history of medicine but also discover how Glasgow itself has changed over the centuries as the standard of medical care reflected how society was developing.

The College is one of the oldest surviving institutions in Scotland, founded in 1599 under a charter granted by James VI of Scotland (later James I of England, Wales and Ireland). Its original purpose was to regulate and improve standards of pharmacy, surgery and medical care in Glasgow and it continues to carry out this role to this day.

Over the course of its long history, the College has amassed thousands of rare medical and surgical instruments. Its collections include historic amputation sets, a cannon shell extracted from a patient's face during the Second World War and part of a femur from the Battle of Waterloo. There are also historic items associated with College members Dr David Livingstone and Joseph Lister, as well as many medical texts from as early as the 16th century.

The library contains a rare partial set of John James Audubon's stunning *The Birds of America*, full sets of which can reach £7 million at auction.

The impressive building occupies several 19th-century houses now joined together. Members are supported through educational workshops and symposia, and the College offers various diplomas and examinations to advance the careers of doctors, surgeons and dentists.

14

THE STATUES
AT NO. 64 WATERLOO STREET

A building influenced by whisky and literature

64 Waterloo Street, G2 7DA
Near Glasgow Central train station

No building in Glasgow has been influenced by literature and whisky as much as No. 64 Waterloo Street. Dating from around 1900, this red sandstone building's façade has three statues representing characters whose identity is lost on modern-day passers-by.

This was once the main Glasgow office and blending site of Wright & Greig, a major force in the drinks business in the late 19th and early 20th centuries. A photograph from 1914 shows a very different street scene to that of today: a long line of men and horse-drawn carts queuing up outside the office, with a caption describing how a record shipment of 12,000 gallons (approx. 545,000 litres) of whisky was about to be sent to Canada.

One of Wright & Greig's best-selling products was Roderick Dhu Highland Whisky, named after a character in Sir Walter Scott's poem *The Lady of the Lake* (1810). In the poem, set by Loch Katrine in the Trossachs, Roderick Dhu is a strong warrior, chief of Clan Alpine, who shelters James Douglas and his daughter Ellen from a vengeful King James V. Part of the plot involves Roderick and the king (travelling incognito as James Fitz-James) seeking the affections of Ellen. Ellen is also a dab hand in a boat, paddling across Loch Katrine.

The impact of the poem was immediate and immense: it sold 25,000 copies within eight months of publication and became popular in many countries. It also helped launch a fascination with Scottish culture and history that drew tourists to the Trossachs to see 'Ellen's Isle'.

Following the book's success, Wright & Greig decided to market their whisky as Roderick Dhu. Adverts and bottle labels featured a black-haired, heroic-looking warrior standing with one arm resting on a rock, the other holding a claymore.

Wright & Greig were also a major employer in Glasgow and owned Dallas Dhu distillery in Forres, Moray.

When construction of a new office began, Wright & Greig wanted to capitalise on their best-selling brand and commissioned sculptures of Roderick Dhu and James Fitz-James for the front of the building, with Ellen high up on the side (holding her paddle). The sculpture of Roderick Dhu is similar to that used in the whisky's packaging, even showing one arm raised up.

Sadly, these great efforts meant little after Wright & Greig went bust in 1919 and the once famous Roderick Dhu whisky disappeared from the nation's pubs. You can still buy it today, however, bottled for Historic Scotland and aimed at tourists and visitors.

'TOBACCO WAREHOUSE' SIGNAGE

15

A rare reminder of the city's tobacco riches

41–59 James Watt Street, G2 8LA
Glasgow Central train station

With its signage reading 'Tobacco Warehouse' up high, the vast, dark building on James Watt Street is a rare physical reminder of the tobacco trade that helped propel Glasgow from a third-rate city into a leading global centre of commerce.

Later run by the Glasgow Tobacco Warehouse Company, the building was constructed for Connell & Co. in 1854, when huge amounts of tobacco were still being imported from America and kept in warehouses such as this along the Clyde before being sent elsewhere. Much of it ended up in the city's many cigarette factories that produced long-forgotten brands such as Tassie du Lux and Glasgow Mix.

By the second half of the 20th century the city's cigarette factories, which had employed thousands of workers, began to disappear. This warehouse therefore stands as a reminder of a lost industrial age, although it also has a connection with the modern age as it is currently used as a document storage centre.

The original tobacco trade in Glasgow began in 1674, when tobacco began to be imported from plantations in the New World. As the 18th century progressed, a group of city merchants took considerable risks in trading with the British Colonies where tobacco was grown on slave plantations in the West Indies and America. These merchants grew so rich that they became known as the Tobacco Lords – or Virginia Dons after the American state where many tobacco plantations were located. The merchants also began to buy their own slave plantations.

As the Clyde faced towards America, Glaswegian ships had a natural advantage over their rivals located in ports further away from the distant plantations.

The Tobacco Lords made even more money after they secured a monopoly to import tobacco into France. By the mid 18th century, they controlled around half of all tobacco imports from America to Europe, and their wealth began to transform Glasgow as new houses, churches and suburbs were built.

The American War of Independence ended the power of the Tobacco Lords, as American merchants muscled in on the trade. Many of the Glaswegian merchants went bust or moved into cotton, continuing to profit from the international slave trade.

A SMOKING CLUB.

Many streets and buildings were subsequently named after the Tobacco Lords or the locations where they had interests in slave plantations – for example, Jamaica Street, Virginia Street and Buchanan Street (named for merchant Andrew Buchanan).

GREEK INSCRIPTIONS
ON THE FORMER ARROL'S BRIDGE

16

Relics of a drowned civilisation

Broomielaw, G1 4NR
St Enoch subway

I f you go down to the bank of the Clyde by Broomielaw, you'll see some orphaned bridge supports (or 'piers') sticking out of the water, some inscribed with Greek letters. This is all that remains of the original four-track, 213-metre-long Caledonian Railway Bridge that crossed the river here and was completed in 1878. It was joined by a second bridge with nine railway tracks in 1905.

The first bridge was built by the legendary Sir William Arrol & Co., a firm that played a key role in Glasgow's industrial heyday and whose work (bridges, cranes and other products) can still be found all over the world.

Arrol's bridge was demolished in 1967 after early changes to the railway signalling system made it redundant. However, it was decided to leave some of the original piers and iron arches in situ, described by architectural writer Robin Ward as looking like 'relics of a drowned civilisation'.

Commissioned to work on the piers in 1990, the artist Ian Hamilton Finlay (1925–2006) added inscriptions in English and Greek taken from Plato's *Republic*, dating from around 375 BC. The Greek reads: ΤΑ ΓΑΡ ΔΗ ΜΕΓΑΛΑ ΠΑΝΤΑ ΕΠΙΣΦΑΛΗ ΚΑΙ ΤΟ ΛΕΓΟΜΕΝΟΝ ΤΑ ΚΑΛΑ ΤΩΙ ΟΝΤΙ ΧΑΛΕΠΑ [All greatness stands firm in the storm].

Finlay was a prominent Scottish poet and artist who was interested in philosophy – in particular, the work of Martin Heidegger (1889–1976). Although Heidegger was a controversial character due to his links to Nazism, Finlay was intrigued by the German philosopher's habit of living in seclusion in a hut in the Black Forest. The English translation quoted above is Heidegger's version of Plato's words, although a more accurate translation is the following: 'All great things are perilous, and it is true, as the proverb says, that beautiful things are hard [to attain].'

Finlay attracted controversy during his career for his own alleged fascination with Nazi symbols, although he successfully sued a Paris-based magazine over its comments on the topic.

Finlay has also left another artistic legacy reflecting a Greek theme: the acclaimed Little Sparta garden located in the Pentland Hills (open to the public). It has been described as his greatest work of art.

'BLOCKADE RUNNERS TO SPAIN' MEMORIAL

A reminder of Glasgow's connections with the Spanish Civil War

South of Clyde Street/East of Glasgow Bridge, G1 4NR
Saint Enoch Subway station

On the north bank of the Clyde are two reminders of Glasgow's often overlooked connections with the Spanish Civil War. One is 'La Pasionaria' – the better known of the two (see box); the other is

a monument unveiled in 2019 which honours Scottish seafarers who defied Franco's blockade of Spanish Republican ports between 1936 and 1939. The bronze figure, by sculptor Frank Casey, shows a sailor giving a warning cry. Underneath is a plaque listing vessels sunk near Republican ports, superimposed on a map of Spain.

The brave actions of British merchant navy ships allowed food, munitions and other supplies to reach anti-Fascist forces in Spain, as well as thousands of ordinary people living in cities such as Barcelona, Bilbao and Madrid. The British government's policy of non-intervention was bravely ignored by many Scottish-owned ships and their crews, and scores of Scots died under attack from Franco's navy.

Between 1936 and 1938, 13 British merchant ships were sunk, and many more were attacked from the air, by submarines and by mines. The subsequent outbreak of the Second World War meant that the losses at sea due to Franco's forces were largely forgotten in the wider conflict. The memorial is the result of fifteen years of campaigning by trade unionists, Frank Casey and the International Brigade Memorial Trust.

At the unveiling, a spokesman from the transport union RMT's Glasgow Shipping Branch commented, 'RMT is pleased that the bravery and solidarity of the seafarers who took huge personal risks to break the Fascist blockade of Spain is at last acknowledged with a permanent memorial in Glasgow eighty years on … Their courage is a beacon and an example to us all.'

'Better to die on your feet than live for ever on your knees'

Nearby is a striking memorial to Glaswegian volunteers who fought and died in the International Brigades while fighting Fascist forces in Spain. The woman portrayed is Dolores Ibárruri, a prominent communist leader with the anti-Franco forces in Spain. Ibárruri (1895–1989) was known as 'La Pasionaria' (the Passionflower) and during the Civil War she made frequent propaganda broadcasts and speeches. The memorial includes her well-known phrase, 'Better to die on your feet than live for ever on your knees.'

The monument was commissioned in 1974 by the International Brigade Association, which seeks to keep alive the story of British volunteers in Spain and maintains over 100 memorials around the country. Designed by Arthur Dooley, the memorial was a controversial project: it was opposed by Conservative councillors, who promised to demolish it when Labour lost control of the council. Ibárruri was invited to the proposed unveiling ceremony but the ceremony was cancelled due to the ongoing political controversy.

VINTAGE OTIS LIFT

A revolutionary lift inside a revolutionary building

The Crystal Palace (Wetherspoon's pub)
Jamaica Street, G1 4QD
Daily 7am–midnight
Glasgow Central train station

Visit the Crystal Palace on Jamaica Street to look at the elevator inside and you may attract some odd looks from those more concerned with drinking and eating. But the vintage lift inside, manufactured by Otis, is a period piece and sits inside an even more important example of innovative architecture in Glasgow.

Dating from 1856, the building was originally called Gardner's Warehouse. Gardner's was then a leading firm of furniture manufacturers and commissioned this design by John Baird. Baird's elegant construction was revolutionary and is today the oldest completely cast-iron fronted commercial building in Britain. His use of cutting-edge materials and techniques produced a warehouse that was superbly lit inside through the huge windows and would have looked stunning to passers-by in the mid-19th century. Gardner's made use of the light to display their wares.

Baird was inspired by Joseph Paxton's huge iron and glass structure constructed for the 1851 Great Exhibition in London's Hyde Park. Paxton's structure was so admired that it was later moved to South London to an area subsequently known as Crystal Palace (hence the name of this pub).

The warehouse was fitted with the then revolutionary Otis elevator, named after Elisha G. Otis. It became famous after the pulley cord was deliberately cut during a public demonstration, proving Otis' innovative safety device would protect passengers. The first Otis lift for public use was ordered in 1857 in New York, so the one you see in Glasgow – imported from the US in the 1850s – dates from the very beginning of the Otis story.

It is easy to overlook the importance of Otis' elevator as we now take his invention for granted. However, it allowed for much taller buildings as humans are not designed to walk up too many flights of stairs. This paved the way for skyscrapers – the term 'skyscraper' emerging out of America in the 1880s to describe buildings over 10 floors in height.

Otis and his invention would help create the famous New York skyline. However, the Crystal Palace – and its lift – is a reminder of an age when Glasgow's business owners and architects were as daring and innovative as anywhere in the world.

REMAINS OF GRAHAMSTON

Glasgow's lost village

Rennie Mackintosh Hotel, 59 Union Street, G1 3RB
Grant Arms, 188–190 Argyle Street, G2 8HA
Beside Glasgow Central train station

Stand outside 59 Union Street (occupied by the Rennie Mackintosh Hotel) and 188–190 Argyle Street (the Grant Arms pub) and you may be looking at the only remaining structures from the fabled lost village of Grahamston.

You won't find Grahamston on any modern map of the city, but if you look at an old map of 1783, you'll see the name. In those days, there wasn't much to see in Grahamston, just a few cottages and small-scale brewers.

The village was named after John Graham 2nd of Dougalston. As the 18th century progressed, the hamlet slowly became absorbed by the city. What had once been open fields were covered with warehouses, breweries and houses. Grahamston even had its own theatre, although that burnt down in 1780 after the magistrate – considering the place immoral – directed the firemen to save houses but to '*Let the Devil's hoose burn!*'.

A map of 1807 shows the main thoroughfare as Alston Street, named after local landowner John Alston of Westerton. Records reveal that Alston Street was a thriving place in the 1850s and 1860s, home to over 2,000 people. Merchants, chimney sweeps, sugar refiners, spirit merchants and coal agents all lived here.

But then, almost overnight, Grahamston disappeared when it was chosen as the location of the Caledonian Railway Company's new station. In the 1870s nearly all the buildings in Grahamston were demolished and over 1,000 residents moved out. The two buildings mentioned above are believed to have survived the redevelopment but no one is entirely sure. The first eight platforms of Glasgow Central Station became operational in 1879.

Despite the destruction, urban legends have begun to circulate suggesting that cobbled streets and abandoned shops still lie beneath the railway station as well as silver and other treasures left behind by their owners.

Today, the remains of Alston Street lie directly underneath platforms 3 and 4 at Central Station. If you want to see the so-called 'secret places' at the station, including old platforms (but not Grahamston's streets!), you can book a tour. See glasgowcentraltours.co.uk for details.

THE *DAILY RECORD* BUILDING

A little-known Mackintosh work

20–26 Renfield Lane, G2 5AR
Glasgow Central train station

Renfield Lane is a dirty, dark and narrow thoroughfare and there is usually absolutely no reason to walk along it. But halfway down, on the north side, you can make out the distinctive tiles of an unusual building that stretches up high above. What you see is the *Daily Record* building, designed by Charles Rennie Mackintosh in 1901. It originally housed *The Daily Record* newspaper.

At the time, Mackintosh was only in his early thirties and reaching his peak as an architect. He had finally been made a partner in the architectural firm of Honeyman & Keppie and his reputation for innovation was starting to gain him recognition among architectural circles in places such as Vienna. He couldn't have known that, in just a dozen or so years, he would be forced to leave Glasgow, sacked from the architectural practice to which he had contributed so much, unable to make a living as an independent architect in his home city.

This was a horrible location for an ambitious architect. It was narrow, dark and rarely visited and gave Mackintosh very little room to manoeuvre. However, he was a perfectionist, using glazed white tiles to maximise light. He also incorporated coloured tiles and a figurative Tree of Life motif. The overall impact is impressive although you have to strain your neck to get a good view.

A lesser architect would not have bothered to include such fine details up high – what was the point when hardly anyone could see them? Mackintosh was a different kind of person, more artist than architect. One of his biographers nevertheless described the building as 'like finding an earring in the gutter'. It was also ahead of its time and to the untrained eye might appear to date from the 1930s instead of the very beginning of the 20th century.

The newspaper moved into the building in 1904. The upper offices were used by journalists and the editorial staff were based on the lower floors, where the newspaper was printed. If you want to peek inside the building, visit the Stereo Café/Bar on the ground floor.

LIBRARY OF ROYAL FACULTY OF PROCURATORS IN GLASGOW

A secret library in the heart of the city

12 Nelson Mandela Place, G2 1BT
glasgowdoorsopendays.org.uk
Open on Doors Open Day
Buchanan Street Subway station

The beautiful, tranquil library of the Royal Faculty of Procurators in Glasgow is only a stone's throw from the bustle of Buchanan Street, but it could hardly contrast more with the city's busiest shopping street. It is a real secret place as it is normally only open to lawyers who are members, many using the library for research purposes. However, the public can visit on Doors Open Day.

The library contains over 80,000 volumes, many of which are of historical importance. Here, the city's lawyers pore over legal texts and articles and conduct research, just as they have done since 1817 when the first library was founded. It provided a place where members could have access to legal books that might be too expensive or too rare for them to access directly.

The 'small library' contains old wooden 'mortification boards' that record the names of past lawyers who have provided bequests for charitable purposes. Visitors can also see the Hill Collection – bequeathed by a past member – which contains historical manuscripts, letters and other documents, including letters from monarchs such as Mary, Queen of Scots.

The legal profession in Glasgow goes back some 1,000 years: the first recorded reference to it dates from 1116. In those times, the Roman Catholic Church controlled many aspects of the legal profession and Scots law was based on Roman law principles. The term 'procurator' is itself derived from the Roman word for law agent. In Glasgow, the profession of procurator developed further, its members having the right to appear in court. To protect their interests, a professional body developed: the Royal Faculty of Procurators.

Although the Royal Faculty has minute books dating back to 1688, it certainly existed before then. 'Royal' was added to the name when King George III granted the body a royal charter in 1796.

A new building for the Faculty was designed in an Italianate style by Charles Wilson, perhaps the finest architect of his era in Glasgow; the library moved here in 1856. Even if you are just passing by, stop to look at the exterior of Wilson's fine building. Above the entrance are sculpted faces that represent distinguished lawyers and judges from the city's past.

One of the most exquisite halls in the West of Scotland

The Glasgow *Herald* described the library in 1857 as 'one of the most exquisite halls in the West of Scotland'.

HOMELESS JESUS SCULPTURE

A poignant reminder of a global problem

Nelson Mandela Place, G1 2JX
Buchanan Street Subway station

Homeless Jesus is a piece of public art that will certainly make you pause if you walk around the back of Tron church on a dark day. On first viewing it appears to be a sculpture of an anonymous homeless person lying on a bench, face covered with a shroud. Only by looking at the feet, which bear the marks of the crucifixion, does it become clear that it is a depiction of Jesus. Space has been deliberately left to allow one person to sit on the bench beside Jesus.

The work of Canadian artist Timothy P. Schmalz (b. 1969), this sculpture has a connection with Canada as it was in Toronto in 2011 that Schmalz saw a homeless person lying on a bench – this inspired him to create the original *Homeless Jesus*, a reminder that anyone can become homeless.

Schmalz, a Roman Catholic, was turned down by two churches when he tried to have *Homeless Jesus* located on their premises. The original sculpture was then installed at the University of Toronto in 2013. Everything changed when *Homeless Jesus* came to the attention of Pope Francis, who visited the statue to bless it and touch its feet. The Pope described it as 'a beautiful piece of art' and since then *Homeless Jesus* has become a worldwide phenomenon.

Some one hundred copies of the work have been installed around the world, from the Vatican to Singapore, New York to Madrid and Buenos Aires. The version of *Homeless Jesus* in Bay Village, Ohio, even made it into the news and was featured in a skit on *Saturday Night Live* after a passer-by thought the statue was a real person in need of help and called 911.

Schmalz has produced other sculptures in the series, taking inspiration from a passage in the Gospel of St Matthew 25:35–45 ('For I was hungry and you gave me something to eat ...'). He once said, 'My purpose is to give Christianity as much visual dignity as possible. Christian sculptures are like visual sermons twenty-four hours a day.'

The statue was brought to Glasgow largely due to the efforts of Father Willy Slavin, who has worked with the city's homeless community for many years.

> Another of Schmalz's creations – *Angels Unawares* – was unveiled in St Peter's Square in Rome in 2019 on the 105th World Migrant and Refugee Day. Again blessed by Pope Francis, it is the first new sculpture in the square for four centuries.

THE BUILDING STONES
OF GLASGOW

Glasgow Rocks!

Nelson Mandela Place, G1 2LL
Buchanan Street Subway station

Everywhere you go in Glasgow, you will see buildings made from stones that are hundreds of millions of years old. However, most people are oblivious to their amazing history.

Two examples can be found side by side in Nelson Mandela Place. First, look at the red sandstone blocks at the entrance to the Chaophraya restaurant. Building stones tend to be either igneous, metamorphic or sedimentary rocks – those here are sedimentary. This means they were formed by layers of sand, mud and pebbles settling down over millions of years under the action of wind or water. One layer often has another stratum of material at a different angle. This creates a visible feature in the resulting rock that is termed cross-bedding. This is evident in the lines you can see on the surface of the red sandstone blocks in the entrance porch.

Much of the red sandstone found in Glasgow was quarried in Dumfries and Ayrshire. The example at the restaurant entrance comes from Locharbriggs, Dumfriesshire. Geologists can even tell that the builders placed certain sections of the cross-bedded sandstone blocks upside down. This example is from the Permian period, so what you are looking at is between 299 and 251 million years old. During this time Scotland was an arid desert and the cross-bedding here was the result of desert sand forming dunes. The red comes from iron in the coating of the original sand grains.

The second example is the Tron Church, opposite the restaurant. In its wall (facing the restaurant), you can see blonde Carboniferous sandstone. This contains dark marks which are the remains of organic plant matter and pebbles. As the building dates from around 1807, this sandstone was probably quarried locally. Much of the blonde sandstone used at this time was quarried from nearby sites such as Cowcaddens, Partick and Kelvingrove. This is much older than the red sandstone you first saw; the Carboniferous period lasted from about 359 to 299 million years ago.

The Geological Society of Glasgow is a great place to find out more about the origin of the stone used in the city's buildings. More information can be found on their website: geologyglasgow.org.uk

HEAD OF A CHINESE MAN WITH A PIGTAIL

A relic of China's past

Former Glasgow Stock Exchange
Nelson Mandela Place & 159 Buchanan Street, G1 3HL
Buchanan Street Subway station

Most people walking down Buchanan Street are looking to buy something or just trying to avoid bumping into other pedestrians. Few notice the statues representing regions of the world high up above their heads, including a Chinese man with a long pigtail. They decorated the façade of the now largely forgotten Glasgow Stock Exchange that once dominated this part of the city.

Scotland used to have its own independent stock exchanges in Glasgow, Edinburgh, Dundee, Greenock and Aberdeen. Founded in 1844, the Glasgow exchange was later housed in this enormous Venetian Gothic-style building that dates from the 1870s.

It was designed by John Burnet (1814–1901), one of Glasgow's most prominent architects, responsible for several other important city buildings such as the Merchants House. Against the Venetian-style arches, look for roundels depicting various industries whose shares were once traded on the exchange.

In the second half of the 20th century, stock exchanges outside London all began to decline as technology improved and the trading of shares became more international. The Glasgow Stock Exchange closed after it was taken over by the London Stock Exchange in the early 1970s. It marked the end of an era as Glasgow once used to have its own financial sector – while never as big as London or Edinburgh, it was still substantial in its own right. Today London's Stock Exchange competes for business with New York and Frankfurt, not Glasgow.

The figures on the Buchanan Street side of the former Stock Exchange represent different peoples from around the world. The Chinese figure has a long pigtail, worn as a symbol of submission to the ruling Chinese dynasty. When the Qing dynasty was overthrown in a republican revolution in 1911, the pigtail (or 'queue') was banned and Western clothes and hair stylings encouraged. This figure hanging over the heads of shoppers is therefore a relic of a lost age in Chinese history.

A few years before the Chinese figure was sculpted, Britain had gone to war twice with China after the Chinese had tried to restrict the imports of opium that had turned millions of their people into addicts.

Glasgow's repurposed police boxes

Six locations across Glasgow:
- *Buchanan Street (city centre)*
- *Cathedral Square (city centre)*
- *Wilson Street (city centre)*
- *Sauchiehall Street (city centre)*
- *Great Western Road at the Botanic Gardens entrance (west end)*
- *London Road at Barrowland Park (east end)*

There are few things more charming than a police box, still freshly painted, a gleaming beacon on an otherwise drab high street. It's one of Glasgow's odd claims to fame that the city boasts more of them than anywhere else across the UK, having maintained and repurposed these odd blue (although not always!) boxes for modern use.

Of course, there's a reason for their enduring appeal: *Doctor Who*. Fans from far and wide love having their pictures taken in front of a real-life TARDIS and Glasgow is in a position to oblige, with several still dotted across the city centre and west end.

But what were the now-defunct big blue boxes really for – and what are they used for today?

Well, first it should be pointed out that they were not always blue. Glasgow, ever keen to do things a bit differently, went against Scotland's uniform blue kiosks until the 1960s, opting instead for pillar-box red. Today, the remaining box in Sauchiehall Street still bears the unique red Glasgow colour.

The real-life TARDISes were made of reinforced concrete, with wooden doors, and the model seen around the city actually bears their name, after local forces tweaked the 1929 design by Gilbert Mackenzie Trench for the London Metropolitan Police and removed one of the four front panels. The three-panel version is now known as the Glasgow box.

The kiosks were introduced in the early 1920s, effectively as miniature police stations. Cops on the beat could use them to call in via a telephone on the inside door, as well as read and file reports inside, or even hold suspects they had nicked until transport arrived. Members of the public could also use the boxes to contact the police in the days before widespread mobile phone use.

Glasgow had more than 300 police boxes in their heyday, but only six remain in locations across the city centre and west end.

Perhaps just as fascinating is their modern-day use, having been repurposed as coffee stands and sandwich spots ... popular places to grab breakfast or lunch on the go.

There's no guarantee that you'll be able to travel through time with just one visit to Glasgow's prime police box locations – but the city's unique eye for retaining remnants of the past and repurposing them for modern use makes for some fascinating and quirky landmarks. It's unlikely that the city council will see fit to exterminate these boxes – nor indeed would the locals stand for it – in years to come.

VESTIGES OF THE 1ST-CLASS WAITING ROOM FOR ANCHOR LINE PASSENGERS

Relics of maritime luxury

The Anchor Line restaurant
12–16 St Vincent Place, G1 2DH
Buchanan Street Subway station

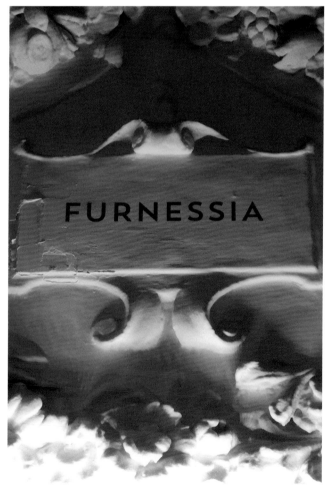

Walk into The Anchor Line restaurant and you are stepping back into history. The plush interior once served as the waiting room for 1st-class passengers travelling with the Anchor Line shipping company. High up on the walls, you can see the names of the Anchor Line's great ships, including the *SS Caledonia*, *Transylvania* and *Furnessia*. The latter was delivered in 1881 and was then the largest ship to have been built in Britain. It sailed regularly between Glasgow and New York.

The entrance gate retains symbols (such as an anchor) of this now largely forgotten shipping line that began in Glasgow in the late 1830s as a merchant shipping firm. It later began to acquire ocean liners, originally taking passengers to the United States, but later extending routes to places such as India, Pakistan and the Mediterranean.

For decades the Anchor Line was important to Glasgow. A company history written in the 1930s recorded how the firm gave 'employment to hundreds of dockers, loading and discharging. Each ship carries between four and five hundred crew, nearly all belonging to or resident around Clydeside. The money circulated for stores and other trade accounts runs into hundreds of thousands of pounds in the year. The welfare of some thousands of people depends on the ships.'

At its peak, the Anchor Line had offices in Glasgow, New York and Dublin as well as a shipbuilding business. It used Yorkhill Quay as its main base on the Clyde until the 1960s, although for many this grand building on St Vincent Street was the public face of the firm. By the First World War, the Anchor Line was running a fleet of 13 ships and many Scots left on one of the firm's vessels to start a new life in distant parts of the British Empire. War had a profound effect on the company: half its fleet was sunk during the First World War, and many other ships were destroyed or damaged during the Second.

The Anchor Line was never as famous as rivals such as Cunard, but it was very identifiably Scottish, its advertising referring to 'Scottish ships and Scottish crew for Scottish passengers'. The growth of airline travel in the second half of the 20th century sounded the company's death knell and it had become defunct by 1980.

The Anchor Building was constructed between 1905 and 1907 to a design by the prolific Scottish architect James Miller (1860–1947), also responsible for interiors on the doomed liner *SS Lusitania*.

NELSON MANDELA BUST

The first place in the world to award Mandela the Freedom of the City

Glasgow City Chambers
82 George Square, G2 1DU
Glasgow Queen Street or Glasgow High Street train station

Hidden deep in the City Chambers, on the right in the foyer, is a bust of Nelson Mandela. It is a reminder of the city's strong connection with the great South African leader who died in 2013 aged 95. But why is it here?

Around the world, streets and buildings are named for him (Glasgow has Mandela Place) but Glasgow was the first place in the world to award him the Freedom of the City. This privilege was granted in 1981, when Mandela was languishing in prison in South Africa and still regarded by many people as a convicted terrorist who did not deserve such a privilege. At the time, it seemed unlikely that he would ever be released, and no one in the wider world even knew what he looked like. It seemed almost unimaginable that he would go on to become President of South Africa and a universally respected global figure.

By awarding the Freedom of the City to Mandela, the Labour-run City Council attracted considerable controversy, particularly as Prime Minister Margaret Thatcher and her Conservative government were refusing to impose rigorous sanctions on the apartheid regime that had imprisoned Mandela. However, other cities in Britain began to follow Glasgow's lead, contributing to a groundswell of popular support for the imprisoned South African. This pro-Mandela movement helped create a global wave of publicity that forced many politicians and influential cultural figures to sit up and take notice for the first time.

Glasgow's Lord Provost Dr Michael Kelly, who had sponsored the award of the Freedom of the City to Mandela, then issued a declaration and a petition for his release. The petition would go on to win support from thousands of mayors in 56 other countries and also the United Nations.

Mandela was finally released from prison in 1990 and by the time he visited Glasgow in October 1993 to formally receive the Freedom of the City, he was one of the most familiar faces in the world. In his speech at the City Chambers, he said, 'While we were physically denied our freedom in the country of our birth, a city 6,000 miles away, and as renowned as Glasgow, refused to accept the legitimacy of the apartheid system, and declared us to be free.' He also spoke to over 10,000 cheering people in George Square, thanking them for their support.

GLASGOW CITY CHAMBERS (28)

Proof of Glasgow's former prosperity as the 'second city of empire'

82 George Street, G2 1DU
0141 287 2000
glasgow.gov.uk
Public tours run Monday–Friday 10.30am and 2.30pm (free)
Glasgow Queen Street station

If there was ever any doubt over Glasgow's former prosperity as the 'second city of empire', a visit to City Chambers settles it. Still, it's a place that few Glaswegians will have set foot in, unless filling in forms and paying parking permits at the John Street entrance to the rear. Watching the festive fireworks display set off from its spired roof each November is as close as many locals get.

What they miss out on, and what councillors and tourists enjoy daily, is a building so opulent and grand that it has been used as a stand-in film set for the Vatican. In fact, it's said that Glasgow City Chambers was built using more marble than the Vatican – and anyone who has seen the film *Heavenly Pursuits* (1986) may recognise its grand staircase, used as a double for the headquarters of the Catholic Church.

Designed by Glasgow architect William Young – who won a competition for the honour – and opened by Queen Victoria in August 1888, the Italian-influenced City Chambers was a symbol of the city's wealth and status as a powerhouse of the British Empire and a growing hub for rich merchants trading goods from around the world.

On the façade, figures depicting Scotland, England, Ireland and Wales stand guard around Queen Victoria on the throne, as well as statues representing the four seasons (so rarely seen in Glasgow!). Inside, the building spans four floors, joined by the imposing white Carrara marble staircase; the first and second levels are also constructed in marble, with the third made of Venetian mosaic tiles.

Linking it all to the bustling city outside is the coat of arms – the bird, the tree, the bell and the fish – displayed in mosaic tiles underfoot as you walk through the revolving doors.

THE TRADES HALL

One of Glasgow's most historic institutions

85 Glassford Street, G1 1UH
0141 552 2418
Book a tour on tradeshouse.org.uk
St Enoch or Buchanan Street Subway station

The Trades Hall, in the heart of the Merchant City district, is a special place: it is the oldest non-religious building in the city still used for its original purpose, i.e. that of a public hall. Completed in 1794, it was designed by Robert Adam, one of the greatest architects of the era.

The public cannot normally visit the Trades Hall (except for being invited to one of the functions held here). However, you can book a place on their tours (see contact details opposite).

This grand building is the home of the Trades House of Glasgow, one of the most historically important institutions in the city. Founded in 1605, its purpose was to act as a federation or central organisation to help individual groups of craftsmen, assist members who had fallen on hard times and defend the rights of the craftsmen against the merchants who had their own organisation.

Fourteen individual professions (known as 'Craft Incorporations' or the 'Crafts') are represented within the Trades House. On the tour, you can visit a small museum that explains the history of the Trades House and the Crafts. For example, the Incorporation of Tailors traces its origins back to 1527 when its members sought to uphold standards of how clothes were made in Glasgow. Other groups include the Bakers, Hammermen, Cordiners, Coopers, Fleshers and Barbers. Legend has it that the Incorporation of Masons trace their origins as far back as 1057, when they were incorporated by Malcolm III of Scotland.

For centuries these Craft Incorporations within the Trades House had a powerful influence over many aspects of commercial life in the city, with their own representatives on the town council.

The Industrial Revolution swept away their powers to control trades and today their activities are largely charitable. They are also involved in education, encouraging school pupils, college and university students through prizes, awards and scholarships. Between them, the Trades House and the 14 Incorporations provide around £750,000 a year in funding, making them one of the largest charitable institutions in Glasgow.

Each Craft of the Incorporations has its own organisational structure and officers and also elects members to the overarching Trades House Trustees.

Anyone can join one of the Crafts, each of which is a charity in its own right. Membership makes a unique and special present for a loved one or colleague (for details, contact the Trades House of Glasgow by phone or via the given website).

THE FOULIS STONE

Two brothers buried under the pavement

98 Ingram Street, G1 1DN
Buchanan Street Subway station

I f you walk along Ingram Street and pass Ramshorn Kirk, look down at your feet. You will see a stone and the initials RF and AF, situated right in the middle of the pavement. Every day people walk by, not realising they are crossing over a burial place.

The initials refer to two brothers: Robert (1707–1776) and Andrew Foulis (1712–1775).

In the 18th century, they were well-known figures in the printing and publishing trade in Glasgow. During their careers, they produced over 500 beautifully designed and printed books, largely aimed at students and academics at the university. As this was during the famous Scottish Enlightenment, the brothers played an important part in the education of those who would develop new ideas and spread them around the world.

The Foulis brothers were interested in the values of education and in 1753 created their own institution, the Glasgow Academy of the Fine Arts, to encourage cultural life in the city. They became so well known for their achievements that Samuel Johnson visited them when he came to Glasgow.

The Church of St David (now popularly called Ramshorn Kirk) was built on this site in 1824, replacing an earlier church. When St David's was built, Ingram Street was widened and this encroached on the cemetery on the south side, so many graves were moved to another section. The exception is the Foulis brothers, who remain stranded under the pavement.

The mort safes of Ramshorn cemetery: designed to keep body snatchers out

The Ramshorn cemetery off Ingram Street is well worth a visit. In operation from 1719 until the early 20th century, the burial ground is notable as the final resting place of rich merchants who used to live in the area. Those interned here include Andrew Buchanan (1690–1759), one of the famous Tobacco Lords (Buchanan Street is named after him).

For many years, corpses were stolen from the graveyard and supplied to surgeons who performed dissections for the benefit of paying medical students. You can see a number of the remaining mort safes: iron cages around the gravestones designed to keep body snatchers out until the bodies had decomposed sufficiently to make them unusable.

GREYFRIARS GARDEN

A secret oasis in the historic heart of Glasgow

Shuttle Street, G1 1QA
Contact: greyfriarsgardenglasgow@gmail.com
High Street train station

Greyfriars Garden is a magical little place, found in the Merchant City, just a stone's throw from the High Street and beside College Street. It's easy to walk past without noticing it (most people do) but it's a real treat, with a wildflower meadow, plants and vegetables growing on raised beds, and greenhouses. There is also a communal shelter, composting facilities, and a lawn and picnic area.

The garden is named for the Franciscan (Grey) Friars, who, in medieval times, were based in a friary standing very near the site of the modern garden. In those days this area, not far from the cathedral, was the heartland of Glasgow before the city spread out in all directions from the 17th century onwards.

The friars' burial ground stood next to the garden. In 2003 an archaeological excavation on neighbouring Shuttle Street found the remains of the 15th-century friary. Some of the original well stones are in the garden today.

The fence on the boundary of the garden (reached along the path leading from the High Street up to Nicholas Street) displays many interesting symbols of the past, including metal shields representing the medieval coats of arms of the City of Glasgow, the University, Bishop Wishart's seal and the Franciscan friary. The stencilled cut-outs show various trades that were important in the city in past centuries, with the vertical timbers representing 10-year periods from the 13th to the 21st century.

The garden was established in 2012 and is usually only open to the public on Open Days. However, you can contact the organisers on the email address opposite to arrange a visit. Outside the fence lies the Deanside Well Garden, which is always open to the public.

Less than 0.4 hectares in size, the garden was founded by members of Greyfriars Garden Association, who were mostly living in the local areas of Drygate, Merchant City and Trongate. The garden helps locals to socialise with each other and learn how to become inner-city gardeners using the 39 individual plots. This 'green lung' in the heart of Glasgow is visited by foxes, rabbits, bees and butterflies.

REMAINS OF THE 'ROTTENROW'

Where generations of Glaswegians came into the world

Rottenrow Gardens, G1 1XUT
High Street train station or Buchanan Street Subway station

The beautiful ruined walls on the north and north-east side of Rottenrow Gardens are all that remains of the 'Rottenrow' – the popular name for the Glasgow Royal Maternity Hospital, which occupied the site from 1860 right up to 4 October 2001, when the last freshly minted Glaswegian was delivered at 4.13 am.

Maternity services were then transferred to the Princess Royal Maternity Hospital and the Rottenrow site was acquired by neighbouring Strathclyde University. The old hospital buildings were demolished and Rottenrow Gardens officially opened in 2004 to coincide with the 40th anniversary of the university's foundation.

The gardens are one of the city's lesser-known green spaces, popular with students during term time and with locals, but rarely visited by Glaswegians from other parts of the city.

The Lock Hospital for venereal diseases

From 1845 the site also housed the notorious Lock Hospital, which specialised in treating sexually transmitted diseases. Between 1870 and 1880 over 4,000 women and girls were admitted, the vast majority drawn from the working class. More than half were 'mill girls' and domestic servants, and around 12 per cent were prostitutes. 'The Lock' was the city's dirty secret, the building designed to look like an ordinary tenement so as not to attract attention. Many of the women and girls here died, the treatment for syphilis being mercury.

NEARBY

In the centre of the gardens stands a modern reminder of the site's history: a 7-metre-high nappy pin sculpture, topped by a bird. Called *Mhtpothta* (Greek for maternity), it was created by the greatly loved Glaswegian sculptor George Wyllie (1921–2012). Wyllie described himself as a 'scul?tor' as he had no formal art training.

CALLANISH SCULPTURE

Glasgow's standing stones

University of Strathclyde, G1 1XN
Glasgow Queen Street/High Street train stations

If you're not a student at Strathclyde University, you might never venture onto the campus. A pity, since it's worth a visit just to see *Callanish* – the megalithic-style steel pillars that dominate one corner.

Erected here in 1974, *Callanish* are the work of Gerald Laing (1936–2011), who was inspired by the famous 5,000-year-old Callanish Stones found on the Isle of Lewis. These prehistoric stones may have been used as a lunar observatory and, according to myth, were created by pagan giants who refused to become Christian.

Laing's modern-day homage consists of 16 free-standing steel structures that also stand 16 feet (5 metres) high and are unlike anything else in the city. Unsurprisingly, they are often described as 'Steelhenge'.

In Laing's own words, the design was created to 'remind the scientifically orientated student that there is a place for the contemplative – and the art student that art must make use of modern scientific materials and scales to remain relevant.'

Gerald Laing had an extraordinary life. Born in Newcastle, he served in the army before ending up as a young artist in New York in the 1960s, where he became friends with figures such as Andy Warhol and Roy Lichtenstein. He became part of the pop art movement, painting Brigitte Bardot among others – seemingly a world away from the mammoth steel constructions you see on the campus. He later lived in a castle in the Highlands, but remained relevant, painting portraits of Amy Winehouse and Kate Moss.

CATHEDRAL HOUSE HOTEL

Glasgow's most haunted hotel

28–32 Cathedral Square, G4 0XA
0141 552 3519
cathedralhouseglasgow.com
High Street train station

I t's said that in order to appreciate Glasgow, you have to look up – architectural gems are there for the taking if you pay enough attention. In the case of the Victorian Cathedral House Hotel, however, it's a case of looking behind the welcoming exterior. There you'll find a fascinating and macabre history.

The hotel sits on the edge of the square, overlooking the Cathedral and bordering the Necropolis, or city of the dead: it wasn't always a happy spot. The building was constructed in 1877 as housing for people released from Duke Street Prison, also known as Bridewell or Glasgow Green Prison. This halfway house is the last remaining evidence of the jail, said to have housed offenders in terrible living conditions until HMP Barlinnie was built to the east in 1882.

Duke Street was used as a prison for women until 1955 and was the site of 12 executions in the 20th century … including the last female to be hanged in Scotland, Susan Newell, who was sentenced to death in 1923 for the murder of a 13-year-old paperboy.

It's little wonder that Cathedral House has earned the title of 'Glasgow's most haunted hotel', with stories of ghosts appearing to staff and spooky unseen bodies brushing past guests on the stairs. The top floor is reputed to be haunted by phantom children and chairs are said to move of their own accord.

The hotel attracts almost as many ghost hunters as it does tourists, although it's unfair to describe it as just a haunted house. The bar is well stocked with the other kind of spirit and the rooms are modern and welcoming.

In 2019 Cathedral House Hotel was taken over by new owners, who have carried out extensive refurbishments, focusing on the period features of the building and providing lofty hospitality to match. Now, it has more of a boutique hotel feel than a haunted hotspot, and owners Shane and Laura McKenzie are keen to promote Cathedral House as a destination for locals and tourists alike.

HEADSTONE OF MARY HILL

The real Mary of Maryhill

Cemetery of Glasgow Cathedral
Castle Street, G4 0QZ
High Street train station

Against a wall tucked away in the cemetery within the precincts of Glasgow Cathedral is a nondescript headstone that hardly anyone notices. However, the person buried here – Mary Hill – is very special as she gave her name to the Maryhill district of Glasgow.

Mary Hill was born in 1730, and her father Hew Hill left her a large estate of rural land then on the outskirts of Glasgow. Named the Gairbraid Estate, the land was developed by Mary and her husband, Captain Robert Graham. Graham had an interesting life: before he met Mary, he had been captured by pirates and held hostage as a slave. Together the couple oversaw the development of a village on their land. Despite several failed ventures, their fortunes took a turn for the better after Parliament agreed in 1768 to place the route of the Forth & Clyde Canal through their estate, causing the value of their land to increase rapidly.

Crucially, the couple required anyone developing the land on their behalf to comply with various restrictions, one of which was that they '[at] all times called [it] the town of Mary Hill'. In an age when women had far fewer rights in society than men, Mary was a formidable, ambitious personality who was determined to follow her own destiny.

When Mary died in 1809, the estate passed to her daughter. In the following years, the hamlet of Maryhill developed into a heavily industrialised district, attracting saw milling, glass works and iron foundries. By 1830 the population had swelled to 3,000 and the village became known as the Venice of the North due to the neighbouring canal system. Maryhill would go on to become a burgh in its own right before being absorbed into Glasgow.

Today tens of thousands of people live in Maryhill. Followers of local trivia might know that the area was used for filming scenes in *Taggart* and *Trainspotting*, and that Hitler's deputy Rudolf Hess was held in the barracks when he arrived in Scotland during the Second World War. Surprisingly few locals – or Glaswegians – are aware that Mary Hill herself is buried in the grounds of the Cathedral.

The most intellectual and obscure graffiti in the city

Glasgow Cathedral
Castle Street, G4 0QZ
Buses: 38, 51, 57

Glasgow Cathedral is full of many treasures, but two inscriptions in particular have both baffled and intrigued generations of Glaswegians.

The first lies at the very rear of the Cathedral, on the north-east side, where you will see an area of wall containing strange, weather-worn inscriptions. It is not known who carved these into the stone, but it appears to be an argumentative dialogue about religion between three different authors, possibly dating from the early 1800s.

One of the inscriptions reads: 'the Philosopher says, "When death is, we are not: the body dies and with it all … "'. Another appears to be a quote from Voltaire, or possibly a Roman philosopher, and another contains words taken from a work by English essayist Joseph Addison (1672–1719).

Were these strange, now greatly worn, carvings in the stonework of the Cathedral the work of drunken students who attended Glasgow University, then located nearby? Surely no one with any respect for the Cathedral would have produced them … they remain the most intellectual and obscure graffiti in the city.

NEARBY

A Hebrew inscription in the crypt

Crypt opening hours vary depending on services. Check the Cathedral website: glasgowcathedral.org/visiting/opening-times

Equally unusual is a Hebrew inscription found in the crypt of the Cathedral on a stone pillar – it's on the south side of the crypt (the third pillar along, counting from the west side). It is thought to date from before 1900 and has only been partially translated. Perhaps a short prayer, it includes the phrase, 'Jehovah is for me, Against me who is? My life is in heaven With those who live forever.'

Whoever crept into the crypt to carve such an obscure text into this pillar? In 1909 a journal speculated that it may have been a 'junior student of Hebrew at the Old College' who was apparently working at speed (due to the sloppiness of the grammar) but no one has ever produced any direct evidence.

MONUMENT TO THE BATTLE OF TEL EL KEBIR

A sphinx in a cathedral

Glasgow Cathedral
Castle Street, G4 0QZ
High Street train station
Buses: 38, 57

Tucked away inside Glasgow Cathedral, the sphinx sitting on top of a monument to the Battle of Tel El Kebir (13 September 1882) is not really a Christian symbol ... It is, however, a reminder of an often forgotten era of Britain's colonial past when it invaded and controlled Egypt. The monument also has a depiction of the battle itself, with soldiers fighting under the watchful eye of General Garnet Wolseley (1833–1913).

The Anglo-Egyptian War of 1882 was sparked off by a national uprising against the regime of Ahmed 'Urabi. The British claimed that 'Urabi's uprising against the Khedive, Tewfik Pasha, threatened British interests and the Suez Canal and sent the navy to bombard Alexandria. The British army then invaded Egypt and had a showdown with 'Urabi's army at the Battle of Tel El Kebir, just over 100 km north-east of Cairo.

Some 13,000 British troops advanced during the night and attacked 'Urabi's much larger force at dawn. The result was an overwhelming victory for the British, who suffered only 57 fatalities compared to around 2,000 killed among 'Urabi's forces. Following the victory, the British army advanced to Cairo ; 'Urabi was captured and sent into exile. The victory signalled a period of effective British control over Egypt that would last until the early 20th century.

One of the British army units that fought at the Battle of Tel El Kebir was the 2nd Battalion Highland Light Infantry (74th Highlanders), which had strong Glasgow connections. The monument inside the Cathedral was erected by 'comrades and friends' of the battalion's officers and enlisted men who died at the battle, and others who lost their lives due to disease during the campaign. Twenty-four men are listed as having died at the battle, while ten died of disease, a ratio showing how the British soldiers suffered in the blisteringly hot and often unhygienic conditions they experienced in the cities and deserts of Egypt.

The sphinx – showing the head of a man on the body of a lion – often guarded the entrances to temples in ancient Egypt. In the 19th century, the sphinx was a common symbol in Freemasonry, so its use in this monument may also reflect Masonic connections of members of the battalion. Below the sphinx, above the poppy flowers (symbol of death), the five-pointed star is also used by Freemasons (although not exclusively): it represents the initiation but also the resurrection.

GYPSY QUEEN MEMORIAL

Coins left for a queen

The Necropolis
Castle Street, G4 0UZ
Daily 7am–dusk
Buses: 38, 41, 57

Among the vast tombs on the north-west side of the Necropolis stands a more modest memorial that doesn't appear very different to dozens of others nearby until you notice an unusual feature: all the gaps in the masonry have been filled with weather-beaten coins.

Get closer and you can read the inscription, which includes the following words: '*CORLINDA LEE, Queen of the Gipsies … she was charitable to the poor. Wherever she pitched her tent she was loved and respected by all.*'

Corlinda Lee was born in Norfolk in 1841, a member of a prominent gypsy family. She married George Smith, an equally well-connected gypsy. As a result, the couple became known within their own community, and far beyond, as the King and Queen of the Gypsies.

In the Victorian Age, gypsies faced prejudice from all quarters, even more so than today. However, Corlinda and her husband helped change how the gypsy community was perceived to some small extent as they formed a travelling group that toured the country. Stopping outside of towns, Corlinda's gypsy encampment put on entertainments and locals were invited to meet (for a fee) the King and Queen of the Gypsies. The highlight was the famous Gypsy Ball, attended by locals and a showcase for the community's musical and dancing skills.

Corlinda Lee's finest hour came when the couple's camp stopped at Dunbar in 1878. It is said that Queen Victoria passed by and acknowledged them, an unprecedented sign of royal approval from one queen to another. Legend has it that Victoria even had her fortune read by Corlinda and took tea with her.

Corlinda would become nationally famous as Queen of the Gypsies before dying in Glasgow in 1900, her special status explaining her burial in such a prestigious cemetery as the Necropolis.

Designed by a well-known mason named Robert Gray, the burial monument once featured a bronze portrait of Corlinda, sadly long since stolen.

The most unusual feature of her burial place are the coins, a traditional offering made by members of the gypsy community when visiting the graves of loved-ones.

GRAVESTONE
OF ALEXANDER MCCALL

'McIntosh's' first work

Glasgow Necropolis, Castle Street, G4 0UZ
Bus 57

In 1888 Charles Rennie McIntosh – later to become Glasgow's most famous architect and designer – was the introverted, artistic, 20-year-old son of a burly Irish-born policeman named William. His father served as chief clerk in the Glasgow police force, working closely with his boss Alexander McCall, the city's chief constable from 1870 to 1888.

When McCall died, it seems that his connection to William McIntosh secured the young Charles his first proper commission: not to design a tearoom or an art school, but McCall's gravestone in the form of this Celtic cross hidden around the back of the Necropolis, far from the grand tombs and mausoleums of the city's most famous figures that dominate the high ground.

At the time Charles – or 'Toshie' – was still studying part-time at the Glasgow School of Art and had an apprenticeship with John Hutchison, long before his glory days working for the practice of Honeyman and Keppie. Toshie still went by the surname McIntosh, only changing it to Mackintosh in 1893.

He was living nearby at the family home at 2 Firpark Terrace in Dennistoun, the back of which lies on the eastern edge of the Necropolis. As a young boy, Toshie must have gazed out over the graves of the Necropolis, never guessing that his first public work would be located there.

There is nothing about the gravestone that looks typically 'Mackintosh' and there are many other similar Celtic-cross designs nearby. However, it is significant as it marks the architect's first public work and the beginning of a career that would make him – at least after his death – internationally famous.

The cross is a reminder that Mackintosh was interested in Celtic imagery and symbolism. It has also been suggested that his later work reflects the influence of the occult on him (and also his wife, Margaret Macdonald). He certainly grew up in an age when an interest in the occult, Celtic and Nordic mythology, spiritualism and Theosophy was widespread. Was he an occultist? Probably not, but the debate about this aspect of his life refuses to disappear.

LADY WELL

A mythical holy well

Ladywell Street, G4 0UU
High Street train station

Hidden down Ladywell Street and opposite the Tennent Caledonian Brewery is the site of the Lady Well, originally an open well used by locals for countless centuries. It was an artesian well, meaning that groundwater came up to the surface under natural pressure, so did not have to be pumped up like a typical well. Its existence can reliably be assumed to pre-date the founding of Glasgow itself and it may have been used by Romans, Druids and other pagans long before the arrival of Christianity.

The Lady Well was just one of a number of 'holy wells' that used to exist in Glasgow, revered in their day for having healing and other spiritual and magical qualities. It is generally assumed to be named after the Virgin Mary, although no one really knows. J. Russel Walker, in an article from 1883, states that the Lady Well was 'so called after a fountain at the bottom of the Craigs ... sacred in Popish times to the Virgin'. Alternatively, it may have been named after a Lady Lochow who lived near the well in medieval times.

What you see today is a structure built by the Council and the Merchants House in the mid-1830s when a wall was built to create a boundary with the new Necropolis cemetery to the rear. The classical structure from 1836 was subsequently restored, again by the Merchants House in 1874 and then by Tennent Caledonian Breweries in 1983.

In 1736 the city still had 16 public wells and Glaswegians continued to use them for fresh water right into the following century. It is part of Glasgow folklore that locals drew water from the Lady Well because they were banned from using the Priest's Well at the Cathedral (that being reserved for the clergy). The Lady Well and others began to be capped during the 19th century as new and more hygienic water supplies became possible with the construction of local reservoirs. No one knows when the Lady Well was finally closed to the public, but it seems to have been the last to remain open in the city.

St Mungo's Well (inside the nearby Cathedral) is still visible, but all the rest have long disappeared. The Lady Well therefore is a rare reminder of Glasgow's past, when obtaining clear water was a daily challenge for most residents and when many people attributed miraculous properties to these wells.

Suffragette stories

Beside 23 Drygate, G4 0XY
High Street train station

People rarely enter the Ladywell housing scheme in Drygate unless they live there or are visiting someone, but at its heart lie the remains of one of the most notorious buildings in Glasgow's history. Beside a convenience store, surrounded by the 1960s housing estate, is a sinister-looking old wall, dated 1871, that was once hidden inside Duke Street Prison. Other smaller sections around the perimeter of the housing scheme give a sense of the huge size of Duke Street Prison before it was demolished in the late 1950s.

The terrible conditions endured by inmates gave the prison a fearful reputation among generations of Glaswegians, just as Barlinnie is regarded as one of the toughest prisons in Britain today. Conditions even inspired a Glasgow street-song which parodied the hymn 'There Is a Happy Land'. The lyrics went: 'There is a happy land, doon Duke Street Jail, Where a' the prisoners stand, tied tae a nail. Ham an' eggs they never see, dirty watter fur yer tea; there they live in misery, God Save the Queen!'

Duke Street began taking prisoners in 1798, and during the mid-19th century was the only prison in Glasgow. Executions took place here right up until 1928 and included the last woman to be hanged in Scotland: Susan Newell in 1923.

After Barlinnie opened in the 1880s, Duke Street became a women-only institution until its closure. It has a place in the story of the struggle for women's rights as many suffragettes were imprisoned here. The suffragette movement was at its most militant between 1912 and 1914, with many followers taking direct action, including arson attacks on houses and pouring acid on postboxes.

Two suffragettes named Ethel Moorhead and Dorothea Chalmers Smith were sent to Duke Street Prison after being caught in 1913 trying to burn down a house in Glasgow. Both went on hunger strike in protest at conditions and Moorhead knocked the prison governor's hat off. Others who went on hunger strike were force-fed or released until they had recovered sufficiently to be imprisoned again. It was a brutal time for many women involved in the struggle and suffragettes were pictured protesting outside the prison. Women's groups continued to criticise prison conditions for decades, contributing to the decision to close down the institution in the 1950s.

MOLENDINAR BURN

Glasgow's lost river

Duke Street, G4 OAJ
High Street train station

Stand facing the old mill at 100 Duke Street and look for some bushes and trees projecting over a low wall on the building's western edge. If you peer over this low wall, you'll see a narrow strip of dirty water. It's not very pretty but it's a section of the mythical Molendinar Burn.

Long before the Clyde became the city's most famous waterway, the Molendinar Burn played a crucial role in the foundation of Glasgow itself: it was on the banks of the burn that St Mungo founded a church in the 6th century. This site (where Glasgow Cathedral stands today) became the original settlement from which the rest of the city grew.

Early settlers used the burn for all manner of purposes: washing clothes, drinking water, transportation and powering mills. The word 'Molendinar' means 'relating to a mill or millers'. The burn may also have featured in ancient pagan rituals and celebrations.

In maps of the early 1800s, the Molendinar Burn is still visible overground, but the city's expansion meant by that by the 1870s much of the burn in the city centre had been covered over and forced into pipes. Having disappeared from view, the significance of the Molendinar Burn also faded from the minds of many Glaswegians. Today it continues to flow, largely forgotten, under the feet of pedestrians. There are a few clues – for example, in the name of nearby Molendinar Street.

The burn begins some 6 km away from Duke Street at Frankfield Loch. It is still overground at this point and remains so as it runs through neighbouring Hogganfield Loch. After that, it starts to disappear. There are a few open stretches but long before the burn reaches the Cathedral, it is entirely underground – except for the small section visible around Duke Street. From here, it flows under Saltmarket before emptying into the Clyde.

HIELAN JESSIE PUB

Glasgow's oldest tenement

374 Gallowgate, G4 0TX
0141 552 0753
Pub open: Monday 11am–11pm, Tuesday & Wednesday 11am–midnight,
Thursday–Saturday 11am–half past midnight, Sunday noon–midnight
Bellgrove train station
Any bus to the Gallowgate/Parkhead

Where is the oldest tenement in Glasgow, you might ask? Well, it's a harder question to answer than you might think because, first, you have to establish what you mean by the word. Officially, the Tenement (Scotland) Act 2004 defines a tenement as 'two or more but separate flats divided from each other horizontally' although most people would argue that modern-day blocks of flats don't fit this description. No matter what you want to call yours, the word tenement is synonymous with Glasgow living.

Today, some 73 per cent of Glaswegians live in a flat of some kind (according to the National Records of Scotland). The most desirable of them are the red or blonde sandstone buildings seen across the city, mainly built in the latter half of the 19th century.

The oldest, then, might not even occur to you as a tenement – but any Glaswegian who knows the historic Gallowgate will recognise the pub, even if they pay little attention to the building above it. The site long occupied by the Hielan Jessie was built in 1771, opposite the barracks of the 17th Highland Regiment – it's named in honour of Jessie Brown, wife of the sergeant of that same regiment. A Victorian heroine, Jessie is famous for spurring on the troops of the British East India Company at the Sepoy Mutiny of 1857. Despite seeing her husband killed, she urged the men around her to fight on after hearing nearby bagpipes, a signal that another Scottish regiment was nearby. The 78th Regiment appeared to save the day and Jessie's name went down in history.

No surprises, then, that the pub directly opposite the regiment's historic home pays tribute to her. The B-listed building remains a popular haunt near another Glasgow favourite, the Barras Market.

Looking up, you could be forgiven for thinking that the four-storey building (the pub occupies the ground floor with two more floors and an attic space above) isn't a tenement at all – after all, we're so used to those sandstone numbers so prized in the west end and south side. But it's worth remembering that tenements of all shapes once existed across the city, though many of them were lost in the 20th century after decades of neglect and disrepair, torn down at the hands of 'progress'.

If we are to take the east end building as a historic tenement, then it can surely lay claim to being one of (if not the) oldest surviving tenements in Glasgow. It's well worth looking up the next time you're wandering along the Gallowgate … and why not head inside for a toast to Hielan Jessie herself?

THE PIPE FACTORY

Innovative arts centre in a historic Barras building

42 Bain Street, G40 2LA
thepipefactory.co.uk
facebook.com/events/1765663683524755/permalink/1824386534319136
Buses: 18, 263

Situated on the edge of the famous Barras market in the east end of the city, the Pipe Factory is a fascinating art space housed in a beautiful historic building dating from 1877. As its name suggests, this was where clay pipes were once made and it is a legacy of the old industries that were once so important to Glasgow. As recently as 2016, however, the Pipe Factory was included on a tour of buildings at risk of being demolished. Thankfully it was saved, and the transformation into the art space you can visit today shows how Glasgow's old spaces can be re-imagined.

The building is just one part of the original pipe factory, with the neighbouring building used for other purposes. They were linked by a two-storey structure whose arch was big enough to allow horses and carts back and forth. In its heyday, the factory had 6 enormous kilns to make the pipes and employed 900 workers. Around 16,000 clay pipes were made each day, most taken by horse and cart down to the Clyde and then exported around the world.

The popularity of clay pipes faded away in the late 1940s and the pipe factory closed in 1950. However, it retains its elegant design, the work of an architect named Matthew Forsyth, who died aged only 30.

Today the Pipe Factory is run by a voluntary committee as a non-profit company. The building is home to several artists who have studios on the old factory floors. The public can visit as the Pipe Factory hosts a regular programme of art events, exhibitions and workshops.

ARCHWAY OF ST ANDREW'S LANE

(45)

A relic of Gallowgate's past

Beside 48 Gallowgate, G1 5AB
and Barrowland Park
Bus stop: Watson Street

Like a computer programme that has been upgraded over time, but which contains traces of obsolete coding, Glasgow contains odd, scattered reminders of an otherwise long-lost past that are hidden in plain sight. One of these lies off Gallowgate and a short street named St Andrew's Lane, lying on the west side of Barrowland Park. The lane serves no obvious purpose and at its short stubby end is a mysterious-looking gated archway that leads under London Road.

If you had stood here in the mid-18th century, the scene would have been very different and made more sense. St Andrew's Lane was far longer, crossing through fields and over the burbling Molendinar Burn before reaching the Church of St Andrew, founded in 1739. However, Glasgow was changing rapidly and, within a few years, its rise as a global industrial centre saw this area transformed by the construction of railways, factories, new residential housing and schools.

In the early 1820s London Street (now London Road – lying to the south of the lane) was constructed, brutally cutting St Andrew's Lane in two. If you walk to the end of the lane to the iron arch under the road, you can read the inscription, 'Erected 1826'. This passage allowed pedestrians to cross under the new road when walking towards the church to the south. For a while, St Andrew's Lane continued to run on the other side of London Road, but this southern section would soon disappear (modern-day James Morrison Street stands approximately on the route).

Other things would change too: the Molendinar Burn was covered over and, in the 1990s, St Andrew's Church became a secular arts centre. For much of the 20th century, the remaining lane and arch under London Road were hidden by a ramshackle market, only revealed again in recent years when the market buildings were demolished to make way for Barrowland Park.

Today the truncated lane is a reminder of the area's past. The gated underpass is closed to the public, serving as a ventilation shaft for the railway underneath: a hidden connection between Glasgow's subterranean secrets and the world we see above the surface.

DOUGLAS GORDON'S 'EMPIRE' SIGN

46

A piece inspired by Hitchcock's Vertigo

Tontine Lane, Bell Street, G14 9SR
High Street train station

t's a fair assumption that the work of any internationally acclaimed artist will be found in a gallery, proudly displayed by the city which nurtured his or her talent. But here in Glasgow, we keep our modern artworks down cobbled lanes, just waiting to surprise passers-by. If ever there was proof that art is for everyone, Douglas Gordon's 'EMPIRE' sign is it.

Tontine Lane is one of those places that few Glaswegians have visited, although many will have heard of it in recent years, thanks to pop-up music and cultural events kickstarted by the 2014 Commonwealth Games. This city-centre spot is just off the beaten track and yet, as with many of the city's 'secret' lanes, you have to know what you're looking for. Heralding your arrival are a few unusual neon signs that look like remnants of old nightclubs or the art deco cinemas Glasgow was once famous for. But one in particular is so much more.

The 'EMPIRE' sign was designed by Turner Prize winner and Glaswegian Douglas Gordon, who was inspired not by his hometown but by a Hitchcock film, connecting Glasgow to Hollywood by way of a cobbled back street in the Merchant City. The piece was inspired by the film *Vertigo*, a mirror image of a sign seen for mere seconds in the classic thriller. One of the 'E's even flickers, a deliberate feature designed to make the sign look authentic.

In *The Merchant City Public Art Trail* (published by Glasgow City Council), Gordon is quoted as saying: 'I liked the fact that I could make an artwork that would not look like an artwork. I could make an object which was a copy of something that doesn't actually exist except in fiction, and the only way you can read it properly is to look in a mirror which is a place that does not really exist either.'

Of course, the word 'empire' has other connotations, especially here in Glasgow. As the 'second city of empire', Glasgow – and in particular, the surrounding Merchant City – bears many remnants of the wealth acquired by the British in centuries past.

The flashing neon is also a nod to Glasgow's cinematic history and the many picture houses across the city which once drew in droves of film fans exchanging jam jars for tickets.

Another Empire sign

The Mitre Bar (which used to sit in nearby Brunswick Street but is now long gone) also had its own Empire sign. It can be seen by visitors to the Riverside Museum, where a recreation of the pub (1895–1930) is on display.

47

CHERUB/SKULL
AT TRON THEATRE

Unusual symbols at a famous theatre

63 Trongate, G1 5HB
Argyle Street train station

Designed by Scottish sculptor Kenny Hunter (b. 1962), two bronze sculptures of a skull and a cherub on the Tron Theatre are probably the most unusual public artworks in Glasgow. Installed in 1997, they were designed to commemorate the Tron building's former use as a place of worship (the cherub) and its current use as a theatre (Yorick's skull from Shakespeare's *Hamlet*).

The cherub, fat and ugly, stands on Trongate and is hard to miss, but the skull is much more difficult to spot, tucked away at the rear of the building on Parnie Street.

The skull is also a reminder that many paranormal activities have been reported within the Tron building, with a hooded figure seen by the Victorian Bar and the ghost of a small girl known as Lily. In 1899 builders discovered corpses under the church when digging the underground line – condemned men had been held here before being executed at Glasgow Cross nearby.

The original church built on this site dated back to 1525. It was burnt down in 1793 by the notorious Hellfire Club whose members were rich, badly behaved young men who preferred debauchery to holiness. However, the steeple survived and was incorporated in a new building dating from 1795 and designed by James Adam, one of the famous Adam family of architects.

While searching for the cherub and skull, also look out for the unusual and substantial figure of St Mungo – the city's patron saint – on the west-facing wall of the Tron steeple by the theatre. It dates from 2001 and was designed by Russian underground artist Eduard Bersudsky whose fascinating Sharmanka Kinetic Theatre is located nearby.

Why the name 'Tron'?

In the past a 'tron' – or weighing beam – was located near here and used for weighing goods entering Glasgow's city walls. Later on, the tron became less important and eventually disappeared from use but the area kept the name Trongate. (The word is derived from an old French word, *tronel*, meaning 'balance'.)

Kenny Hunter is also responsible for the much admired *Citizen Firefighter* statue outside Glasgow Central train station.

BRITANNIA PANOPTICON

48

The world's oldest surviving music hall

117 Trongate, G1 5HD
0141 553 0840
britanniapanopticon.org
Tuesday–Saturday, midday–5pm. Also open for special evening events
Argyle Street rail or St Enoch Subway station

Keys, you can lose – even a car can be misplaced. But how can you lose an entire theatre? The Britannia Panopticon is the world's oldest

surviving music hall: a shrine to the bawdy, working-class entertainment your Victorian ancestors may well have attended.

You'll find a single doorway entrance down an alleyway off the Trongate. A historical-themed gift shop points the way, as does a plaque dedicated to Mr Stan Laurel. But the place was shut up until 1997 – unless you count the chickens that roosted there during the Second World War.

Back in the 1850s, more than a thousand people would squeeze in up to four times a day to watch dancing girls, comedians and singers try to impress ... and 'impress' is the word. Legend has it that those who rediscovered the theatre found it full of metal rivets – the weapon of choice for tough crowds who weren't enjoying the act onstage and used scraps from the Clyde shipyards to pelt the performers off again.

In 1896 electricity came to Glasgow and the Britannia Theatre was one of the first buildings to light up, allowing audiences access to the new big thing: moving pictures.

The arrival of grand theatres like the King's and the Theatre Royal meant that the Panopticon became old hat to some in Glasgow but the Trongate attraction kept on going for years to come. From carnival games to a zoo billed as 'Noah's Ark', complete with bears and monkeys, it seems that just about every form of entertainment was wheeled out to pack in the masses.

The Britannia Panopticon's fortunes changed with the arrival of cinemas in Glasgow, and the ground floor of the building was turned into shop space – the upper auditorium was shielded from view by a lowered ceiling. It remained virtually untouched for decades until a group of volunteers came along and created a charitable trust. Now, Glaswegians can watch music-hall performances as in the days of old or take in a silent movie. They can even spend the night, looking for the ghosts of performers once booed off stage.

Visitors can tour the old hall and see the work being done to restore it to its former glory ... if they wander far enough off the well-trodden Trongate to find Glasgow's once-forgotten theatre.

The place where Stan Laurel, of Laurel and Hardy, started

A young boy of 16 made his debut on the Panopticon stage, having been introduced to the proprietor by his dad, who ran a music hall nearby. His name was Arthur Stanley Jefferson – and perhaps it was surviving that tough crowd which spurred him on to conquer Hollywood as Stan Laurel, of Laurel and Hardy.

ARANDORA STAR MEMORIAL

A tragic event that affected hundreds of Scots-Italians in the city

Italian Cloister Garden
St Andrew's Cathedral
196 Clyde Street, G1 4JY
Normally open from dawn to dusk each day
St Enoch Subway station

On the east side of St Andrew's Cathedral (completed in 1816), the Italian Cloister Garden contains at its centre a memorial to a tragic event that directly affected hundreds of Scots-Italians in the city.

On 2 July 1940 a ship named the *SS Arandora Star* was transporting internees and prisoners of war to Canada when it was sunk by a German U-boat off the coast of Ireland. The resulting loss of life was immense: well over 400 Italian and 243 German 'enemy aliens' out of an estimated total of around 800 victims.

The impact on the Scots-Italian community in the city was devastating as nearly everyone lost someone they knew. This tight-knit community had formed in the late 19th century when Italian immigrants arrived in Glasgow seeking a better life. Many became involved in opening cafes, selling fish and chips and ice cream, and by the 1930s the community was of a substantial size. However, the outbreak of the Second World War saw many Italian businesses attacked by other Glaswegians, angry at supposed links between the community and the Fascist regime of Mussolini.

Scots-Italians were frequently forced out of business and many were interned under 'anti-alien laws' even though their siblings, children or parents were serving Britain in the armed forces.

Over the following years, memorials to the tragedy have been erected in several locations, from Liverpool to Barga in Italy. The last survivor in Scotland was Rando Bertoia, resident of the Gorbals and a retired watchmaker, who died in 2013 aged 93. His cousin Luigi was drowned when the ship went down. Bertoia attended the ceremony to open the Memorial Garden in 2011 alongside Archbishop Mario Conti and First Minister Alex Salmond. Representatives from towns in Tuscany and the Lazio region also attended, these being the areas from where most of the Italians who first settled in Glasgow came.

Designed by an Italian, Giulia Chiarini, the memorial features striking mirror plinths and a wall containing the names of all the Scots-Italians who died on the *Arandora Star*. The inscriptions on the monument were chosen from the Gospels and the great Italian poets. The 200-year-old olive tree at its centre was a gift from the people of Tuscany.

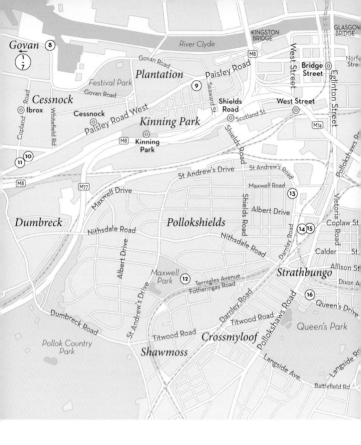

Glasgow South

LITERARY FACES

A misspelling on Govan Road

577–581 Govan Road, G51 2AS
Govan Subway station

On a quiet stretch of Govan Road stands a Victorian sandstone building with six curious faces staring down. Four are famous: William Caxton, who introduced the printing press to Britain; Scottish literary giants Robert Burns and Sir Walter Scott; and Johannes Gutenberg, another pioneer of the printing press, best known for mass-producing copies of the Bible.

The other two faces will be unknown to most passers-by: they are John and Jane Cossar, who opened a print shop in Govan in the 1870s. The couple went on to publish the *Govan Chronicle* in 1875; it became the *Govan Press* newspaper three years later. The Govan Press was printed to the rear of the newspaper office building facing Govan Road. On the top floor of the office, the words 'Press Buildings' are still visible.

John Cossar died in 1890 but Jane continued to run the business (which later included other newspapers) until her own death in 1926. The office building and the busts of the couple on the façade were completed a few months before John's death – it must have been odd for Jane to look up at her dead husband's face every time she went to work over the following decades. The family firm and the Govan Press newspaper closed down in 1983 although the title was later revived.

One of the Cossars' sons, Thomas, invented the Cossar printing press in the early 20th century. It was so successful that it was exported around the British empire and used to print newspapers from Australia to Beirut with such exotic names as the *Whanganui Chronicle* (New Zealand) and the *Rangoon Mirror* (Burma).

National Museums Scotland has in its collections a Cossar printing press that was originally installed in Crieff in 1907 – it is claimed to have inspired the machine that prints *The Quibbler* in *Harry Potter and the Deathly Hallows*.

Sadly, none of these achievements prevented a typo on the front of the building, as 'Gutenberg' should only have one 't'!

FORMER GOVAN POLICE STATION

STATION

Victorian cells with a Nazi connection

Orkney Street Enterprise Centre
18 Orkney Street, G51 2BX
Ring to arrange a visit: 0141 274 3333
Govan Subway station

Built in 1867, the former Govan police station hosted generations of troublemakers. Many were drunks who spent a night there after overindulging in Govan's numerous pubs, but the cells also held hardened criminals such as gangland legend Jimmy Boyle. After lying derelict for many years, the building is now home to the Enterprise Centre, a hub for various organisations, but the historic police cells have been carefully preserved.

The most famous prisoner was Rudolf Hess, Hitler's closest ally. This extraordinary story begins in the First World War when Hess, a young Bavarian infantryman, fought at Ypres and on the Somme. When the war ended, the young man was disillusioned about his prospects in post-war Germany and became involved in radical, right-wing anti-Semitic groups. Hess first heard Hitler speak in 1920, joined the Nazi party and became the Führer's devoted friend.

Hess served time in prison with Hitler in the 1920s; his loyalty would later be rewarded when the Nazi leader made his friend his deputy. By the time that the Second World War broke out, however, Hess had been sidelined by men such as Himmler. Probably driven by resentment at no longer being Hitler's favourite, he set off on the strangest mission of the war.

Hess flew alone from Germany on 10 May 1941, planning to land at the country estate of the Duke of Hamilton in South Lanarkshire. Hess thought he could negotiate a secret peace treaty between Germany and Britain, and that the Duke – who had met senior Nazis in Germany before the war – would help. His mission ended when the plane ran out of fuel and he parachuted out, landing in Eaglesham. After being captured, Hess is thought to have been held briefly in Govan police station before being moved to Maryhill barracks. He would spend the rest of his life in gaol, dying at Spandau prison in Berlin after committing suicide in 1987 aged 93.

The police station originally had 40 cells that could hold 120 prisoners. It was also part of Govan Burgh Hall when Govan was still independent of Glasgow. The historic cells are attractive locations for television companies and several episodes of *Rebus* (with actor Ken Stott playing the iconic detective created by Ian Rankin) were filmed here.

GOVAN CAT SCULPTURE

③

The legendary cat that saved Govan

Rear of Brechin's Bar (Burleigh Street side)
803 Govan Rd, G51 3DJ

On the Burleigh Street side of Brechin's Bar is an odd sculpture high up on the wall – hard to make out at first, but it's a curled-up cat. Why is it there? According to a Govan legend, centuries ago the village was plagued by rats that had arrived on ships carrying flax for the local weavers. Villagers brought in a cat to tackle the rats and it did a great job until – finally – it came up against the king rat. Both cat and rat died in the ensuing battle, but Govan was saved from the rat infestation.

The legend was immortalised in this building, erected in 1894. It's proof, if you needed it, that Govanites have a good sense of humour.

Brechin's is another Govan institution, so make sure to have a beer here when you're in the area. You'll be following in the steps of the famous philosopher Noam Chomsky, who visited the pub in 1990 after attending a conference nearby.

A Govan resident named Anne Melvin wrote a poem entitled 'The Govan Cat', which includes these lines:

There is a place called Govan
Which was overrun by rats
In fact there were so many
They outnumbered dogs and cats
They terrified the people
And made them ill at ease
You can hardly blame them
For they carried such disease ...

THE GOVAN STONES

One of Glasgow's most interesting and little-known attractions

Govan Old Parish Church
866 Govan Road, G51 3UU
0141 440 2466
thegovanstones.org.uk
Daily 1pm–4pm (1 April–31 October)
Free
Govan Subway Station or Govan Ferry from Riverside Museum (summer service)

ourists arriving in any major city will expect to see its landmarks signposted and its areas of interest advertised and mapped out in guidebooks. But few Glaswegians – never mind visitors – would think of going to Govan for an educational day out. And it's a trick missed by many, because the former burgh, now a major residential area to the south of the River Clyde, holds one of Glasgow's most interesting, and still under-appreciated, attractions.

Govan Old Church houses an impressive collection of early medieval stones dating back to the 9th and 11th centuries. They are thought to commemorate the rulers of the kingdom of Strathclyde – in a nutshell,

there may be kings buried in this earthy corner of Glasgow!

It's a far cry from Govan's reputation in the 20th and 21st centuries: from industrial hub, full of hard-working men and hard-drinking pubs, to an area facing hardship in the decline of shipbuilding on the Clyde.

Govan is not a place often marketed to tourists, and it's doubtful that many Glaswegians would jump straight to it when planning a day out. But for anyone interested in the history of the city, this southside neighbourhood holds more than intricately carved stones. The settlement dates back to AD 500 and a small wooden church built on the 'little hill', or 'Govan'. The area was part of the kingdom of Dumbarton, ruled by the Clyde Britons until the Picts and Northumbrians invaded in the 700s, and it later became part of the kingdom of Strathclyde.

Govan Old Church makes the most of its wonderful collection, with all 31 medieval monuments – from crosses and cross shafts to five hogback stones – displayed in full view of the congregation and any visitors who want to wander around. The Govan Sarcophagus, dated to the mid to late 800s, is particularly impressive. Carved from a single block of stone, its scenic panels are still visible, including a warrior hunting on horseback – thought to be a symbol of Christianity. It's not known who the sarcophagus was meant to commemorate, but it must have been intended for someone of grand status.

The rest of the collection – known as the Govan School – are believed to have been carved between 900 and 1100 and include the hogback burial monuments. These Norse-influenced stones are typically found in areas settled by Vikings, most prevalent in the north of England and the Borders – but with five of them on display, Govan has the largest known collection in Scotland. Its array of hogbacks and intricate crosses are believed to indicate a cemetery of high status, perhaps even burial plots reserved for kings.

All of this is available to view for free on the Govan Stone trail once you know where to look.

Since 2012, efforts have been made to put Govan on the map for more than shipbuilding, and work is ongoing to investigate the Govan Stones and their significance on the local, national and international level.

The church and its remarkable slice of medieval history are well worth a trip across the Clyde, whether you ride the Glasgow Subway to Govan or take a more unusual method of transport. The Riverside Museum lies just across the river, on the north bank of the Clyde, and is a major tourist attraction. But few visitors know that, during the summer months, the volunteer-led Govan Ferry runs between both banks, dropping off just a short walk away from Old Govan Church. It's a pleasant way to cross from Partick to Govan, and the small boat provides another welcome gateway to one of Glasgow's hidden gems.

FAIRFIELD HERITAGE CENTRE

*Memories of a time when the Clyde produced
a quarter of all the world's ships*

1048 Govan Road, G51 4XS
Monday–Friday 1pm–4pm (times vary: fairfieldgovan.co.uk)
Govan Subway station

If you stand outside the former Fairfield shipbuilding offices on Govan Road, you'll see the striking figures of a shipwright and an engineer dating from the 1890s. They look out proudly, blue-collar workers who are rarely depicted among Glasgow's late-Victorian public sculptures. They mirror the figures of two workers that adorn the old Govan burgh coat of arms, a testament to how vital the shipbuilding industry was to this area.

Behind them is the Fairfield Heritage Centre, housed in the finest example of a shipbuilding office found anywhere in Britain. Many Glaswegians are aware that their city once had a significant shipbuilding industry, but this was decades ago. It's not easy today to get a sense of its importance.

The Fairfield Heritage Centre is the best place to go if you want to understand this heritage. The centre has a wealth of information on the shipbuilding industry, with videos, exhibitions and numerous artefacts such as detailed models of ships used to help construct the full-size versions.

The heyday for Glasgow's shipbuilding was the early 1900s, when the Clyde produced around a quarter of all the new ships being made around the world – an astonishing figure. Fairfield contributed to this by constructing ocean liners, tankers, merchant ships and warships for the Royal Navy. Their ships were put into service around the world, particularly in far-flung parts of the British Empire such as Australia, Canada and South Africa.

The origins of the Fairfield business go back to 1834, when Charles Randolph founded an engineering firm. He was joined in the 1850s by a brilliant engineer named John Elder, who helped spearhead a drive into the making of innovative marine engines. Elder led the firm when it set up a shipbuilding business in Govan in 1864 and it became Glasgow's second-largest producer of ships by tonnage. After Elder died in 1869, the company was named after him. It continued to thrive for many years, producing 55 warships between 1870 and 1909.

Fairfield's later became the Fairfield Shipbuilding and Engineering Company and was bought and sold a number of times in the 20th century. Today BAE Systems continues to build naval vessels in Govan, so Fairfield is not just a museum piece.

The building was designed by John Keppie (whose firm employed Charles Rennie Mackintosh). It was completed in 1891 and had ship and engine drawing offices and a magnificent boardroom.

GOVAN COAT OF ARMS

Reminder of a lost age of independence

Elder Park Library
228A Langlands Road, G51 3TZ
Govan Subway station

Above the entrance to Govan Library stand the statues of two men separated by a shield and surrounded by other heraldic symbols. This is a rare study in stone of Govan's coat of arms and is a legacy of when it was not only independent of Glasgow but the seventh largest burgh in Scotland.

The men represent an engineer and a ship's carpenter, while a vessel lies on the stocks between them. When the coat of arms was registered in 1884, shipbuilding was the most significant industry in the area, and members of the local burgh authority were keen to ensure that this was reflected in the official coat of arms and burgh seal.

Above are other heraldic figures and symbols that are much older: a helmet and stars, thought to have been taken from the coat of arms of William Rowand of Bellahouston and his descendants, the Rowans of Homefauldhead. They had links with the area long before industrialisation changed Govan. Underneath is the burgh's Latin motto *Nihil Sine Labore*, meaning 'Nothing without hard work' – fitting for Govan, given how much industry was once located here.

By the time Govan became an independent burgh in 1864, it had already been transformed over the previous half-century from a village dominated by fishermen and silk workers into one of the great shipbuilding centres of Britain. But thousands of working-class people who had flocked to Govan for jobs did not share in the wealth generated through the local shipbuilding and other industries founded here, despite the grand buildings that remain from that era: the Govan Library, the Pearce Institute and the former burgh town hall in particular.

Govan Library (opened in 1903) was designed by the esteemed Glasgow architect Sir John James Burnet and resulted from a bequest by Isabella Elder (1828–1905), a wealthy philanthropist and the widow of John Elder, owner of the famous Fairfield shipbuilding firm in Govan. The coat of arms above the library's entrance was a symbol of civic pride. However, it would not last long as Glasgow wanted to incorporate burghs such as Govan and Partick into the city. Many wealthy local people voted against the proposed amalgamation in a public vote, but it was the poor who helped consign Govan's independent status to the history books.

Glasgow promised working-class people in Govan that they would pay lower taxes if they became part of the wider city; they would also enjoy new amenities such as washhouses, public baths and a hall. These promises helped swing the result and in 1912 Govan finally became part of Glasgow. This coat of arms was just one of many things that became obsolete overnight.

RELICS OF GOVAN'S PAST

Memories of the city's rural and shipbuilding past

Elder Park
Govan Road, G51
Govan Subway station

A quiet spot on the north-east side of the city, Elder Park contains two surprising relics of Govan's past. The first is a grotty derelict building (hidden behind railings) that is all that remains of Fairfield Farm. Part of the original farmhouse, it dates from around 1850. It is significant as there is nothing else in Govan – other than its old church – that would be recognisable to a Govanite from the mid-1800s were they to be transported through time to the 21st century.

By the late 19th century, the farm had been sold to one of Govan's major shipbuilding firms. However, while the farm disappeared, its name lived on in the famous Fairfield Shipbuilding and Engineering Company. Other lands within the old farm estate were incorporated into Elder Park, opened in 1885. Govan became one of the most heavily industrialised places in Britain, so to have such a reminder of a rural, agricultural past is incredibly rare in central Glasgow. It only survived because it was used for years as an amenity building within the park. Its future remains uncertain as it is on the 'at risk' register.

Near the old farmhouse, an Italianate portico stands like an ancient Roman ruin. Its origins go back to the 1790s, when the Mansion House on the nearby Linthouse Estate was built for the City Chamberlain, James Spreull. The famous architect Robert Adam is thought to have been involved in its design. The mansion was added to by further building in the early 1800s and was later acquired, together with the 32-acre (0.13 sq. km) Linthouse Estate, by the shipbuilders Alexander Stephen & Sons. Situated approximately where the south side of the Clyde Tunnel is today, Stephen's was where the young Billy Connolly worked. The Mansion House was used as offices by Stephen's before being demolished in 1921. The sole remains of this once leading shipbuilding firm were brought here soon afterwards and re-erected.

GOVAN GRAVING DOCKS

An abandoned historical place loved by urban explorers

Govan Road, G51
Site closed to the public – views from Glasgow Science Centre on south bank of the Clyde or Clydeside Distillery on the north
Govan Subway station
Any bus to Govan Cross

There are few derelict sites more hotly debated here in Glasgow than Govan Graving Docks. Once the epicentre of the river Clyde's industrious shipbuilding legacy, the ruin now stands to the west of the new media hub Pacific Quay, just before busy Govan Cross, closed off from the public and yet beloved of urban explorers who know where to slip through the fence.

It has been a film set for everything from BBC comedy *Limmy's Show* to Hollywood blockbuster *1917*. It has even been an open-air theatre.

And it has been a battleground off-site too, with local campaigners long trying to stop developers turning this Clydeside spot into housing. Plans for a maritime museum on the site remain on the table while these

discussions are ongoing although the future of Govan Graving Docks is, as ever, up for debate.

Still, the ruined tower on the edge of the Clyde's south bank remains a fixture on the skyline for many – and to lose it completely would change the face of Govan's waterfront ... for the worse, in the opinion of many Glaswegians.

The dry docks were built for the Clyde Navigation Trust: the first opened in 1875 followed by two more in 1886 and 1898. The famous Clyde steamers were the trade here. Govan Docks were used for winter overhauls and refits, and the docks allowed for inspection and repair of the hulls of ships. That work continued until 1988, when the graving docks were abandoned and left derelict. Since then, the area has been subject to vandalism, including several fires lit in the shell of the main building.

The Clyde Docks Preservation Initiative continues to push for the restoration of one of the remaining remnants of Glasgow's shipbuilding heritage. In 2017 they commissioned a documentary by Fablevision Studios on the dock's history, present plight and potential future. The film is available to watch online and gives a fascinating insight into the former docks. It also sheds light on the site's importance to the people who live and work nearby today.

As for exploring the place, enthusiasts continue to get access now and then ... unless the site has been taken over by another film crew, as in the summer of 2019 when *1917* brought Hollywood to the banks of the Clyde.

The future of Govan Graving Docks may remain unclear, but if you're passing the river on the north bank, between the Riverside Museum and the Clydeside Distillery, and you notice an interesting old ruin on the other side of the water, then bear in mind that you're looking at traces of old Glasgow – and a site which is still hugely important to history buffs and modern-day Govanites alike.

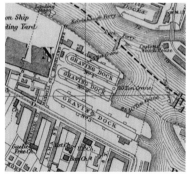

WHISKY CASKS OF THE OLD TOLL BAR

The ultimate hidden historical gem

1 Paisley Road West, G51 1LF
facebook.com/theoldtollbarglasgow
0141 258 4830
Monday–Thursday 11am–11pm, Friday & Saturday 11am–midnight,
Sunday 12.30pm–11pm
Kinning Park Subway station

It's true that Glasgow isn't short of bars, with several laying claim to the title of the city's oldest remaining pub, and many dotted around the city centre. Head off the beaten track to a spot less frequented by tourists, however, and you'll find the ultimate hidden historical gem with curious links to Glasgow's famous shipbuilding past: a Victorian 'palace' pub with many of its original fixtures still intact.

The building, a three-storey Glasgow tenement with the pub below, dates back to 1860. For years, its heritage was hidden behind 20th-century optics and blaring fruit machines, but a 2016 refurbishment returned the pub to its former glory, courtesy of its new owner.

From outside, The Old Toll Bar in Kinning Park looks like a traditional, but perhaps ordinary, pub. But behind those heavy double doors lies a stunning curved bar built by the very hands which once clasped pints there after a hard day's graft on the Clydeside shipyards.

The polished, dark woodwork throughout and panelled ceiling gleam in the candlelight, and the stained-glass windows are a nod to the style of the famous Glasgow tenements – some located directly above. The ornate gantry has four beautiful whisky casks surrounding a mirror centrepiece and clock, and the walls are decorated with more stunning mirrors showing old advertisements for port, brandy, champagne and claret.

According to the current landlord, Mido Soliman, the intricate woodwork would have been carried out by shipyard workers. With fierce competition among 19th-century publicans to have the most beautiful watering hole, bars in the area are thought to have been built using spare materials from the yards and putting Glasgow's proven craftsmanship to good use – all in return for payment in liquid form.

Historical photos and dates important to The Old Toll Bar now line the walls, testament to a Victorian pub so lovingly maintained. But this is no museum to a Glasgow that once was: the bar is a thriving community hub, hosting regular music sessions and events and serving up a great selection of drinks ... without the inflated price tag you might expect from similar establishments elsewhere.

It's a name unlikely to register with many Glaswegians beyond real ale enthusiasts and locals, but an afternoon spent at The Old Toll Bar provides as much insight into the history of Glasgow as a day wandering the city museums.

GLASGOW CLIMBING CENTRE

Climb – quite literally – to the heavens in a former church

534 Paisley Road West, G51 1RN
0141 427 9550
glasgowclimbingcentre.com
Monday–Friday 11am–10pm, Saturday & Sundat 9am–6pm
Adult climbing sessions start at £7; entry to café free
Ibrox Subway station

Churches across Glasgow have been repurposed for a variety of reasons; some have even been divided up and turned into upmarket properties. Oran Mor, Cottiers, The Lansdowne – all these former holy places are now entertainment venues.

But there are a few former churches where you can climb – quite literally – to the heavens. Head south to Ibrox and you'll find the old church, still boasting its ornate spire and period features but with huge changes behind those arched doors. That's because this Victorian building is now a climbing centre ... an unlikely but unique spot for Glasgow adventure seekers.

It was originally built as a Presbyterian church, no more than a simple wood structure dating back to 1865. The present building is a replacement, enlarged by Bruce & Hay in 1890. Since then, it has been a United Free place of worship and a Methodist church – until the 1990s, when it became the Glasgow Climbing Centre.

Today, the stained glass remains intact and the wooden beams are as ornate as any church in the city ... but between the floor and the ceiling stretch numerous climbing walls, all regularly dotted with harnessed and helmeted adventurers.

Climbers come from further afield to experience a truly unique indoor wall, but the centre caters for complete novices too, so Glaswegians who have never heard of the place can experience the adrenaline rush for themselves. In fact, there are 50 individual routes around the old church, from vertical ascents to overhanging boulders.

A well-kept secret café

If climbing sounds too exhausting, then there are other ways to reach the top: a spiral staircase in the middle of all the action leads to the excellent Balcony Café, a well-kept secret among Glasgow's foodie community.

Lunch or dinner in 'the gods' of the church, watching climbers scale the sides, is an experience every Glaswegian should have at least once – they just have to find the place first.

Historic distance marker

Opposite 564–566 Paisley Road West, G51 1RF
Ibrox Subway station
Buses: 9, 10

In Ibrox, hidden behind a tree and hardly visible against a grimy wall, lies a historic mile marker. The stone, which is only about knee height, is hard to read because of centuries of weather corrosion. On one side it says, '5 miles to Paisley, 25 miles to Greenock'; on the other, '2 miles to Glasgow'.

Old maps show that such distance markers were found all around Glasgow and outlying areas – they were important as travellers then had no satnav, smartphones or road maps to help them plan their journeys. Many a weary traveller walking in the rain or going by horse and cart would have stopped here to work out how many hours they still had to go.

Most of these historic distance markers have disappeared over the last century or so, victims of redevelopment and the city's expansion. No one knows when this one dates from, but it seems likely it was placed here in the late 18th or early 19th century when this district was not even within the city limits.

The road then would have been largely surrounded by fields and near a building called 'Two Mile House' that has long since been demolished. In the past, the importance of distance also led to other buildings and inns around here being called 'Three Mile House' and 'Half Way House' (the latter marking the midway point between Glasgow and Paisley).

THE MASONIC SYMBOLS OF POLLOKSHIELDS BURGH HALL

The hidden Masonic symbols of a southside gem

70 Glencairn Drive, G41 4LL
0141 423 8858
pollokshieldsburghhall.com
Open by appointment
Maxwell Park train station

The leafy suburb of Pollokshields is far removed from the tenement blocks and industrial shipyards so often captured in photos of old Glasgow. West Pollokshields is old money: a neighbourhood of vast mansions and Victorian villas surrounded by parks. It's no surprise, then, that Victorian southsiders required a meeting hall as grand as Pollokshields Burgh Hall.

The land was given to the burgh by Sir John Stirling Maxwell in 1887. Glasgow architect Henry Edward Clifford was chosen to design it, leaning on 17th-century Scottish Renaissance styles for a red sandstone building that's still impressive and imposing today.

A community centre of sorts this may be – it's used as a polling station, public meeting room and wedding venue – but the Burgh Hall is a far cry from others across the city, surrounded by the greenery of Maxwell Park and boasting an 18-metre-high tower and stunning stained glass.

This place is a treasure trove of hidden historic and architectural gems and there's something new to spot in the stonework on every visit. Assuming that wedding guests have better things to do with their day, here are just some of the interesting snippets of the past maintained by Pollokshields Burgh Hall Trust today.

The commissioners of the burgh used the place as a Masonic lodge, and the connection remains to this day, with the emblems of Freemasonry dotted throughout.

The stained-glass windows were gifted by wealthy residents of Pollokshields and they range from the practical – a 1935 window with the Corporation of Glasgow symbol – to the more philosophical memorial window dedicated to the lodge's 'departed brethren'.

Sir John Stirling Maxwell's influence is felt here too. Another window reads 'Do Good While the Holly is Green', a nod to the greenery outside and Sir John's love of nature.

Windows in the smaller halls provide further links to the lodge, including one dedicated to St John the Baptist, patron saint of Freemasonry.

Whether you're keen to delve into hidden symbols or just a nature lover looking for a leafy corner of the city, Pollokshields Burgh Hall is the historical gift that keeps on giving, far beyond the burgh it was intended to serve.

FORMER MILLAR & LANG ART PUBLISHERS OFFICES

An obscure rival to Mackintosh

46–50 Darnley Street, Pollockshields
Pollockshields East train station
Buses: 3, 4, 6, 7, 37

On the southside of Glasgow, the former offices of Millar & Lang Art Publishers were once housed in this extraordinary building that should be far better known. It looks like a classic design by Charles Rennie Mackintosh, and if it was, it would be celebrated in tourist guides. However, it is not, and stands a little shabby and ignored in Pollockshields, its architect so obscure that architectural guides do not even mention his date of death.

The extraordinary interior features a wealth of stunning imagery, from mermaids to bats and dragons, with beautiful stained glass (by William Gibson Morton) in the reception and a wealth of detail elsewhere: mosaics, wall tiles, doors, woodwork. The exterior is also superb, particularly the

dragon on the water pipe and the mermaid on the first floor. It is a wonderful example of the 'Glasgow Style', a term given to the innovative group of young artists in the city who between the early 1890s and 1914 forged their own distinctive approach to design. Mackintosh is today the most famous member of this group, which comprised around 75 people.

The offices are the work of David Bennet Dobson (b. 1871), still a young man when the main building was completed in 1902. Dobson was a contemporary of Mackintosh, and they both studied at the Glasgow School of Art during the same period. Dobson became associated with progressive, Art Nouveau designs and the Glasgow Style.

Dobson was working with the architectural practice of John Gordon when he received this commission from Millar & Lang. They were well known for their postcards (including some that poked fun at suffragettes – including their being force-fed), humorous books and other publications with an artistic flavour. If Dobson had continued in this vein, could he have been as well known as Mackintosh today? Possibly, but his career fizzled out: he set up his own practice, designed a few other buildings but disappeared after 1908 (he is thought to have left Glasgow). Even Mackintosh struggled to find enough commissions in Glasgow to stay solvent, so Dobson's fate was not unusual.

GLASGOW GURDWARAS

Two fascinating new landmarks

37 Albert Drive, G41 2PE
0141 423 8288 – glasgowgurdwara.org
Every day
Tours available by appointment: book by phone or online
Pollokshields East train station

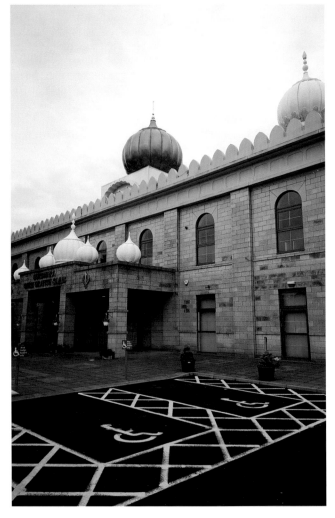

They say that if you want to appreciate Glasgow, then you have to look up – usually referring to the ornate Georgian and Victorian buildings that have long loomed over the city's busy streets. But there are two new additions to the skyline which deserve attention in their own right ... and they are a world away from the Gothic revival of Glasgow University or the opulent displays of wealth over in the Merchant City.

The Glasgow Gurdwara Guru Granth Sahib Sikh Sabha, in Pollokshields, was the first of two Sikh temples to take shape. It was, in fact, Scotland's first purpose-built Sikh Gurdwara – for the last 50 years, the south side's Sikh community had used an old Victorian villa nearby.

The temple opened in April 2013, creating a fascinating new landmark next door to arts venue Tramway and its celebrated Hidden Garden (see page 222). To escape the bustle of the city, head for the garden one sunny afternoon and you'll see blue skies and the golden dome of the religious building over the wall – a beacon marking the fact that all are welcome to the Gurdwara, regardless of belief.

The Visit Scotland-accredited tour includes an overview of the day-to-day workings of the Gurdwara, a viewing of the Darbar Hall (prayer room), information on the Sikh faith and an invitation to the Langar Hall, where free food is served daily. Perhaps one of the most fascinating tenets of the Sikh faith is this community kitchen where anyone, regardless of religion, caste, gender or status, is welcome to sit down and share a vegetarian meal.

Whether you're an architectural fan or just enjoy meeting new people, a chance to look inside one of Glasgow's newest, most prominent buildings is surely the ultimate hidden gem, a year-long Doors Open Day ... and one which many Glaswegians don't yet know about.

The Glasgow Central Gurdwara Singh Sabha followed suit across the river, opening in 2016 and providing another gilded point of interest on the skyline. Although it's tucked away beyond Charing Cross on a quiet street, the city's second golden dome stands out from any high vantage point, and heralds a proud new multicultural direction for Glasgow.

THE HIDDEN GARDENS

An oasis away from overwhelming city life

Tramway, 25a Albert Drive, G41 2PE
0141 433 2722
thehiddengardens.org.uk
April–September: Tuesday–Thursday 10am–5pm, Friday & Saturday 10am–7pm, Sunday midday–6pm
School summer holidays: Tuesday–Saturday 10am–7pm, Sunday midday–6pm
October–March: Tuesday–Friday 10am–3.30pm, Saturday & Sunday midday–3.30pm
Free
Pollokshields East train station
Buses 3, 38 and 57 from city centre to Pollokshaws Road

Glasgow is blessed with an abundance of parks and green spaces, so it comes as no surprise that the city's nickname is the 'Dear, Green Place'. Among those grassy spots are secluded, private greens, many of them created especially for the rich neighbours surrounding them: head to Hillhead, Dowanhill or Park and you'll see countless private gardens, albeit from the other side of a locked gate.

So what are the rest of us supposed to do? We could make do with Kelvingrove or Queen's Park and put up with the throngs of people lining the grass on a rare sunny day in Glasgow. Or we could look to another hidden garden, designed with the people in mind: you know, those of us who won't keep it under lock and key.

Head to Tramway, in the south of the city, for the ultimate secluded spot: Glasgow's Hidden Gardens. The venue is one of the city's premiere arts hubs, housing Scottish Ballet and serving up art, theatre, dance and more on a weekly basis. Not bad for an old tram shed far from the city-centre buzz. If you've been walking by it without going in for years, then you're missing out. Just as impressive as the billing is what lies behind the building.

In 2003 public arts organisation NVA came up with the idea of a unique public greenspace, run by the community of Pollokshields and offering every available path to inner peace, all by way of a stunning secret garden. People of all cultures and faiths have been using it ever since, whether it's for a weekly exercise group or pitching in with the gardening. Community groups keep it thriving while the Hidden Gardens remain open to all, come rain or shine.

It's difficult to describe the atmosphere other than saying that it really is a little oasis away from overwhelming city life. The noise of the streets outside falls away and the greenery and winding paths seem the perfect antidote to Scotland's biggest city, wonderful as it is.

Still, there are reminders of Glasgow's past throughout. Designed to reflect the site's changing uses, the large brick chimney towering overhead gives a nod to industry and the fact that designers kept the tram lines intact is a nice touch.

Is there a better spot to enjoy your lunch on a sunny day? The Hidden Gardens certainly seem up there with the best, while retaining a distinct Glasgow feel and providing a place of tranquillity for Glaswegians from all walks of life.

QUEEN'S PARK GOVANHILL CHURCH OF SCOTLAND STAINED-GLASS WINDOWS

Glasgow's unlikely Holocaust heroine

170 Queen's Drive, G42 8QZ
0141 423 3654
qpgpc.com
Queen's Park train station

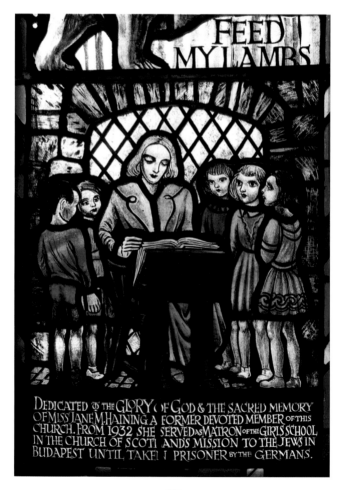

FEED MY LAMBS

DEDICATED TO THE GLORY OF GOD & THE SACRED MEMORY OF MISS JANE M.HAINING A FORMER DEVOTED MEMBER OF THIS CHURCH. FROM 1932 SHE SERVED AS MATRON OF THE GIRLS SCHOOL IN THE CHURCH OF SCOTLANDS MISSION TO THE JEWS IN BUDAPEST UNTIL TAKEN PRISONER BY THE GERMANS.

Ten Scots were murdered at the Nazi extermination camp at Auschwitz-Birkenau. One of them was Jane Haining, who went to Budapest as matron of a boarding school for Jewish and Christian girls but never returned.

Born in 1897, Jane is considered a hero in her native Dumfries and Galloway, but it was Glasgow, and a life she had built there as an adult, that she left for Hungary in 1932. She had settled in Glasgow's Southside in 1917, taking a secretarial job in Paisley and attending church at Queen's Park. There, she was inspired to join the Scottish Mission School in Budapest.

As tensions mounted in Europe, Jane refused to leave the 400 children in her care. The Church of Scotland wrote repeated letters asking her to come home but her response was: 'If these children need me in days of sunshine, how much more do they need me in these days of darkness?' Nazi troops marched into Budapest in March 1944. Jane's days in Hungary were numbered and she was arrested by the Gestapo in May.

Records suggest that Jane lasted two months at Auschwitz. Her death certificate, marked 17 July, simply reads: 'cachexia following intestinal catarrh'. Holocaust researchers continue to debate how she died, some suggesting she was one of the many sent to the gas chambers and others that she starved to death.

For members of the congregation of Queen's Park (now joined with the nearby Govanhill church), it's a story passed down through the generations and forever recorded by two stained-glass windows. Jane's former minister, Reverend J.L. Craig, dedicated two windows to her in June 1948: 'To the glory of God and the sacred memory of Miss Jane M Haining, a former devoted member of this church. From 1932 she served as matron of the girls school in the Church of Scotland's mission to the Jews in Budapest until taken prisoner by the Germans.'

The only Scot officially recognised as 'Righteous Among The Nations'

Jane Haining remains the only Scot officially recognised as 'Righteous Among The Nations' at Yad Vashem, the World Holocaust Remembrance Center, in Jerusalem. There are also memorials to her in Budapest.

CATHKIN PARK'S EMPTY FOOTBALL TERRACES

Ghostly remains of a lost football team

58–82 Florida Ave, G42 8XG
Crosshill train station

Although it has a distinguished place in the history of football in Scotland, and Glasgow in particular, Cathkin Park on the southside is not that well known to many Glaswegians. If you enter the park for the first time, you may have no idea how important it once was but the clues are there on all three sides: eerily empty football terraces once crammed full of spectators.

Cathkin Park used to be Hampden Park, which you may find confusing. However, there have in fact been three Hampden Parks. The first, used between 1873 and 1883, was situated not far away, and when it closed the site was built over (currently occupied by railway lines and Hampden bowling club). The second Hampden Park (renamed Cathkin Park) was used between 1883 and 1903, but as football became more popular, it was not suitable for future use as a national stadium. The third (and current) Hampden Park opened in 1903.

To confuse matters further, the name Hampden (deemed so important by Scotland's football authority that it has been used for three different locations) is actually taken from the surname of an Englishman named John Hampden who fought for Oliver Cromwell in the 17th century.

Whilst Cathkin Park was no longer where the national side played after 1903, it remained a key venue in Scottish football. It became the home of one of Glasgow's long-lost teams – Third Lanark. They stayed here until the club closed down more than 60 years later.

Few Glaswegians under a certain age have heard of Third Lanark. However, they were once a major force in the game: at their peak, up to 15,000 spectators crowded the now deserted terraces. Founded in 1872 by members of a military outfit, the Third Lanarkshire Rifle Volunteers (3rd LRV), Third Lanark were known as the Hi-Hi. They were a founder member of the Scottish Football Association in 1873. The team toured South America in the early 1920s, playing Argentina, won the Scottish Cup twice (in 1889 and 1905) and finished third in the league in 1961.

Third Lanark even beat the mighty Celtic 2–1 to win the Glasgow Cup in 1963 (the final was played at Hampden Park). Sadly, poor financial management doomed the club to extinction and it finally folded in 1967. The team's many fans were heartbroken and were forced to shift their allegiance to other Glasgow teams. Had the club been run better, could Third Lanark be sharing titles with Celtic and Rangers today? We will never know, and every year that passes means there are fewer people around who stood on the terraces at Cathkin Park and saw the team play. Sadly, Third Lanark have become a footnote in Scottish football history and the club's closure also ended Cathkin Park's connections with top-level football after 80 years.

SOUTHERN NECROPOLIS

Glasgow's other city of the dead

Caledonia Road, G5 0JQ
0141 287 3961
southernnecropolis.co.uk
No. 21 First Bus towards East Kilbride Gardenhall

Comedian Billy Connolly once said, 'Glasgow's a bit like Nashville, Tennessee: it doesn't care much for the living, but it really looks after the dead.' Although he was referring to the Necropolis which twists around Glasgow Cathedral, in the oldest quarter of the city, there's another lesser-known site to the south of the Clyde.

The Southern Necropolis remains relatively unchanged as the surrounding area continues to evolve. Notorious neighbourhood the Gorbals was once known for its slums and its razor gangs, but now new housing developments are springing up in the wake of high rises.

Opened in 1840, the Southern Necropolis has 250,000 burial plots across 21 acres (8.5 hectares). Those interred there include Alexander 'Greek' Thomson, the celebrated Glasgow architect; Sir Thomas Lipton of Lipton's Tea fame; and John Begg, nephew of Robert Burns. There is, however, one carved stone that the Necropolis is famous for, particularly for those who like a good ghost story.

The White Lady marks the resting place of a carpet manufacturer named John S. Smith, as well as his wife Magdalene and housekeeper Mary McNaughton. The veiled statue may be weather-beaten and missing a nose, but the stone she stands beside remembers the tragic deaths of Magdalene and Mary, who walked in front of a tramcar on Queen's Drive on their way back from church one rainy day in 1933. Local legend has it that the White Lady is not as stationary as she seems: some say she turns her head as passers-by cross the grave, prompting many to keep an eye on her until out of sight.

The iron-toothed vampire who was picking off local children

The area is perhaps most famous for the 'true story' of the Gorbals Vampire and the events of September 1954. With rumours circulating that an iron-toothed vampire was picking off local children, some 100 weans decided to take action. Only in Glasgow! These plucky youngsters were found patrolling the Southern Necropolis by night, armed with stakes, axes, knives and garlic, ready to take on the Gorbals Vampire if he was brave enough to show his face.

The story has amused locals and interested the wider world for years. It even spawned a comic-book series, created by an American artist fascinated by the spooky tale.

In the end, they never did find the vampire, but the chances of spotting him, along with numerous other points of interest, are well worth a visit to the lesser-known Gorbals cemetery where it all happened (even if it's in the safety of daylight).

GORBALS BOYS SCULPTURE

Street art inspired by Glasgow's favourite photographer

Queen Elizabeth Gardens, Gorbals, G5 0SS
Bridge Street Subway station

Queen Elizabeth Gardens in the Gorbals is the location of a poignant and unusual public artwork. In the middle of the pavement stand three bronze statutes of small boys wearing high heels. If you have no idea about the inspiration behind *Gorbals Boys*, this may seem a very

strange sculpture; however, the meaning is clear as it captures the innocence and fun-loving spirit of kids just playing together.

The sculpture is based on a particular moment in 1963 when three young boys in the Gorbals were playing in their mother's high heels on Kidston Street. The Gorbals then looked very different to today, dominated by streets of tenements that have since been swept away in redevelopment schemes. The boys were from working-class families and grew up in an era when playing in the street was entirely normal.

By chance, the Italian-born photographer Oscar Marzaroli saw the boys and took a picture of them playing, a photo that would become one of his most iconic images. His ability to capture the essence of working-class life in Glasgow in the second half of the 20th century made him the city's most popular photographer and today exhibitions of his work attract visitors from all walks of life.

Three decades after the picture was taken, artist Liz Peden came across it in a book of Marzaroli's photographs. It inspired her to recreate the scene in bronze as part of the Gorbals Arts Project.

Peden used three local boys named Nicky, Joe and Lee to stand in high heels and model for her. She described how it 'made me think about the whole scenario we have had in this area of being a real hard area, and here were three boys in their mother's shoes. And it was how kids did play, they played in the streets. It made me smile and it made me reminisce.'

Nicola Sturgeon, then Deputy First Minister of Scotland, unveiled the sculpture in 2008. Sadly, Marzaroli had died in 1988 but his widow Anne attended the ceremony.

Most sculptures of people in the city represent famous politicians, soldiers or artists, but this is a rare example of ordinary people being immortalised.

The boys in the photograph have never been identified despite efforts to track them down. Perhaps one day an elderly man will pass by here and remember a moment of joyful play decades before.

TOOLS OF THE TRADE
IN THE GORBALS ROSE GARDEN

Historic garden in the heart of New Gorbals

G5 0RS
Bridge Street Subway station

Mention the Gorbals to most people and it's likely to conjure up a host of images, few of them positive. However, the whole area has been transformed many times over the years, beginning in the late 18th century when a rural village of a few hundred inhabitants gradually turned into an industrial centre whose slum tenements became infamous around the world. Later, many of the industries disappeared, as did the tenements when they were replaced by tower blocks. More recently, the

tower blocks have been torn down and much more pleasing modern housing constructed.

Given all these enormous changes, the Gorbals Rose Garden is a rare survivor of the original village. This site was opened as the Gorbals burial ground in 1715. Today the old gravestones have been moved to the edge of the garden by the walls, but they provide a fascinating and rare link to the past. A few gravestones display the tools of the trade used by the deceased who, when alive, were proud of their status as skilled workmen.

In the 19th century many of Glasgow's older burial grounds were built over or closed as they were full. The opening of the nearby Southern Necropolis in 1840 provided a new site where locals could be laid to rest. The bodies buried here were moved away in the 1960s.

The garden is part of an ongoing regeneration of the Gorbals. It has a community orchard of 76 fruit trees, run by locals, and is thought to be the first public orchard of its kind in Scotland.

There is also an unusual war memorial in the shape of a rose, dedicated to local Gorbals men who died fighting for their country. It mainly honours James Stokes, who won a posthumous Victoria Cross in 1945 after leading several charges against the German machine-gun posts (he died from his wounds).

The McLennan Arch: the last remaining element of the old Assembly Rooms in Ingram Street

The McLennan Arch is the last remaining element of the old Assembly Rooms in Ingram Street, on which construction started in 1796.

The Merchant City building was demolished in 1892 – to make room for a post office, which hardly seems as grand – and the arch was moved as a stand-alone structure to Monteith Row in Calton. It then made its way to Greendyke Street, at the north side of Glasgow Green, in 1922.

Glaswegians with a long-enough memory may remember the arch being moved to its current home, off the city's famous Saltmarket, in 1991 – a year on from the City of Culture accolade which marked a move towards the vibrant city we know today.

So where does the name come from? It is not, as you might think, named after some grand architect. Robert and James Adams designed the Assembly Rooms, and presumably the arch with it.

Anyone who stopped long enough to admire it, however, may have noticed the inscription: 'This Arch was presented to his fellow citizens by Bailie James McLennan J.P.'

CALTON BURIAL GROUND

Martyrs of Scotland's first organised strike

309–341 Abercromby Street, G40 2DD
Open all day
Bridgeton train station

The Calton Burial Ground is a small, secluded and normally deserted cemetery in the city's east end – it was used for burials from the late 18th century until the 1870s. This atmospheric place, recently renovated, contains a memorial to those who died in a tragic confrontation that became a historic event in the nation's trade-union movement.

In 1787 many of those living in this district were employed as weavers and were experiencing the birth pangs of the Industrial Revolution. When told that their wages for weaving muslin were being reduced, it caused widespread anger. Over a period of several months, there were a number of strikes, the first such organised strikes to take place in Scotland.

On 3 September 1787 a large number of angry weavers went on a march, intending to assemble by the Cathedral. When they reached Drygate Bridge by the Gallowgate, they were blocked by soldiers from the 39th Regiment of Foot, who opened fire. Six of the marchers were killed, and three were buried here: James Page, Alexander Miller and James Ainsley. The tragic end to the march signalled a growing polarisation between workers and industrialists in Glasgow, one that would poison industrial relations for generations to come. It would also earn the city a reputation as being home to radical elements that were not afraid to challenge the status quo.

Also look out for the burial marker of the Rev. James Smith (1807–1874): in the mid-19th century, this Scot moved to America and served for a few years as minister of a church in Springfield (Illinois). A young man named Abraham Lincoln and his parents attended the church and knew Smith well, long before Lincoln became a famous politician. In 1861 Smith came to Washington as a guest of Lincoln, now President

of the United States and grappling with the outbreak of the Civil War. Smith used the goodwill he had built up in the past to obtain a posting as US consul to Scotland, with Lincoln's agreement. Smith died in Scotland just a few years after Lincoln was assassinated.

GLASGOW WOMEN'S LIBRARY

A collection quite unlike anything else in the UK

23 Landressy Street, G40 1BP
0141 550 2267
Monday, Tuesday, Wednesday & Friday 9.30am–5pm, Thursday 9.30am–
7.30pm, Saturday noon–4pm. Closed Sunday
Museum and archive collections: by appointment
Bridgeton train station
Any bus to Bridgeton Cross

On the edge of the east end, in a grand former library of Bridgeton, you'll find a collection quite unlike anything else in the UK. That's because Glasgow Women's Library (GWL) is the only accredited library of its kind, dedicated to 'women's lives, histories and achievements' – and celebrating the ordinary women of Glasgow with regular talks and events.

For those who already know it, it's a treasure trove of information and insights ... and if you don't, then here's why it's worth hopping on a train to Bridgeton soon.

The lending library – whose collection has been donated entirely by members of the public – makes up the greatest part of GWL, providing inspiration for generations of female readers and writers present and future. The place also houses museum and archive collections, available to view by appointment, including extensive material on LGBT history, from the 1920s to present day.

For anyone with an interest in feminism, and the struggles feminists have faced in the last century, the archive material is a fascinating delve into life in the UK – and beyond – amid commonplace, garden-variety misogyny, looking at everything from outdated adverts to domestic artefacts owned by the 'woman of the house'. In short, it's a treasure trove of information for anyone interested in female history in general, as well as the women of Glasgow.

But perhaps the most interesting activity at the centre is its programme of regular events, from Drama Queen theatre groups to poetry readings, networks for women of colour and exhibitions which tie in to an overall theme of showcasing the work of women.

GWL first opened its doors in 1991, aiming to put the spotlight on women's contributions to the city's history, particularly following Glasgow's role in 1990 as European City of Culture. At the time, it was a tiny shopfront in Garnethill.

The B-listed building now housing the Glasgow Women's Library is the result of Scottish government grants and ongoing public donations, as well as support from a number of high-profile Scottish women, Nicola Sturgeon included. And the place continues to grow ...

Whether for academics or for keen observers of social history, this may be one of the most important, if undervalued, museum resources in Glasgow – but for women of the east end and beyond, it has become a real hub of activity worthy of the grand building it now calls home.

RUTHERGLEN BOUNDARY STONES

Relics of an ancient burgh

Farme Cross – between Farmeloan Road & Smith Terrace, G73 1BB
Rutherglen train station

Hidden away on a quiet street is a small, seemingly insignificant-looking stone where the date 1709 can still be seen. It once had a very important function as a boundary stone for the Royal Burgh of Rutherglen.

Rutherglen is among the oldest Royal Burghs in Scotland and was granted this privilege by a charter issued by King David I in 1126. The status of Royal Burgh granted its residents many privileges, including the right to hold a market, normally held at the market (or 'mercat') cross.

But why bother to place hundreds of boundary stones around a perimeter of over 24 km? In the days before maps, or at least accurate ones, the inhabitants of Rutherglen wanted to protect the common land held by the burgh from being encroached upon by neighbouring

districts and other landowners. Boundaries often followed natural, easily identifiable features like rivers and burns.

In these far-off times, burgesses were citizens granted certain privileges by the burgh. According to tradition, every new burgess was required to provide at their own expense a carved stone to be placed along the boundary. The stone was marked with their initials and the year of its erection. Every three years or so, the Provost and other burgh officials would walk the boundary of the burgh to inspect the stones.

This became both a practical and a symbolic event, a time for the community to celebrate and recognise the independence and character of their own burgh. In the past, the common land was called the 'merk' or 'mark', so the boundary markers were known as 'merkstones'. The procession around them, either on foot or by horseback, was called the 'riding' or 'redding', leading to the Scots term 'redding of the marches'. This ceremonial procession was found throughout Scotland in the past and is still carried out today in several locations around the country.

The Rutherglen Heritage Society has recently examined the notebook of Jasper Brown, Rutherglen's Town Officer in the 1920s, who made notes about each boundary stone during the redding of the marches in which he took part. Research by the Society has helped uncover many boundary stones that had long been forgotten. The oldest known one dates from 1574, but they were probably first put in place much earlier, perhaps as far back as the foundation of the Royal Burgh in the 12th century, when the redding of the marches is thought to have begun.

There used to be around 370 stones, but today only around 57 are still in situ, often hidden away in private gardens, in parks or beside roads. They are a fascinating reminder of the strong community spirit and history of once-independent burghs such as Rutherglen before they were consumed by Glasgow.

To find out more about the location of the stones past and present, visit the Rutherglen Heritage Society's website: rutherglenheritage.wixsite.com/website-46/royalty-boundary-stones

N

A809
A81
Milngavie
A807
A810
A810
A879
A809
②
Clydebank
A82
Bearsden
A739
③
A82
A81
①
A814
p. 12
B808
④
A8
⑤
Renfrew
River Clyde
A82
p. 92
Glasgow
A741
A739
Airport
GLASGOW
✈
M8
⑥⑦
A741
M8
Paisley
A761
A736
A761
M77
A77
A726
⑧
p. 192
A736
B768
B774
⑬
B771
M77
Pollock
Country ⑫
Park A77
⑨
B769
⑭
Barrhead
A726
Giffock
⑩
⑪
B767
A736
A727
Clarkston
B771
B769
B766
M77
B759
Newton Mearns
B767
A77

0 1 2 km

Glasgow - To the West and South

POSSIL MARSH NATURE RESERVE

A hidden nature reserve in north Glasgow

scottishwildlifetrust.org.uk/reserve/possil-marsh/
*Best accessed from Forth & Clyde canal tow path or park the car at Lambhill
Stables (11 Canal Bank North, G22 6RD)*

If you want to visit a loch and experience swamp, marsh and fen less
than 6 km from the centre of Glasgow, head north to Possil Marsh.
Sandwiched between Lambhill Cemetery and the Forth & Clyde canal,
it's not that easy to access if you haven't been before but it's worth a visit
if you're seeking respite from the busy streets of Glasgow. As it's spread
over some 32 hectares, you can walk here and not pass a single other
person.

At its heart is Possil Loch, which accounts for about 15 per cent of
the total site, the rest being fen, swamp, damp grassland, dry meadow
and birch and willow scrubland. The site has long been classified as a

Site of Special Scientific Interest (SSSI) on account of its diverse ecology and wildlife.

The marsh attracts breeding birds such as reed buntings, moorhens and water rails between May and July, and in the colder months around 150 species of birds winter here.

If you take the path around the perimeter, you will walk past thousands of wildflowers. The best time to visit is May to July if you're interested in breeding birds, May to August to see the wildflowers and October to March to see wildfowl.

The first meteorite recorded as landing in Scotland

On 5 April 1804 a meteorite landed near the reserve and became known as the High Possil meteorite. Only three others have been recorded since then. There is a memorial stone to commemorate the event. Today, the meteorite is held in the Hunterian Collection in Glasgow.

RELICS OF ANTONINE WALL ②

One of the few physical reminders of Scotland's most impressive feat of engineering

New Kilpatrick Cemetery, Bearsden, G61 2BB
Open 24 hours
Hillfoot train station

STONE BASE OF THE ANTONINE WALL
BUILT BY THE ROMANS FROM FORTH TO CLYDE A.D.142

In the suburban New Kilpatrick Cemetery lie the remains of a substantial section of the Roman Antonine Wall that once stretched right across the narrowest part of Scotland. Very rarely visited, the stone remains were once part of a rampart on the wall and are one of the few physical reminders of perhaps the most impressive feat of engineering in Scotland's history.

The wall was built right across central Scotland from the Firth of Clyde to the Firth of Forth, a distance of just under 65 km. It was begun in AD 142 during the reign of Emperor Antoninus Pius and was punctuated by 16 forts and smaller 'fortlets'. The construction took 12 years and was largely undertaken by Roman soldiers. The Hunterian Museum in Glasgow contains a wealth of artefacts and construction stones taken from the route of the wall, many identifying the individual legions involved in the building works.

At the time the wall was built, the Romans were still determined to control the difficult Caledonian tribes; however, for reasons not fully understood, they abandoned the wall about eight years after it was completed. In a major strategic retreat, the Romans withdrew their forces south of the much more famous Hadrian's Wall, which became their new northern frontier. (The retreat may have been because it was too expensive for the Romans to keep troops so far north along the Antonine Wall, tying up thousands of soldiers from around the empire.)

The Antonine Wall was largely made of turf, stacked up on a stone rampart. As a result, most of it has eroded over the centuries. By contrast, Hadrian's Wall was mainly built of stone, so much more has been preserved. However, there are many places in Scotland where you can see the outline of the Antonine Wall as it wound its way across the country, together with substantial remains of forts and the old military road that ran parallel to the wall.

Despite being abandoned, the Antonine Wall was reoccupied by Emperor Septimius Severus in AD 208. This second occupation by the Romans only lasted a short time, however, and the wall was then abandoned for ever.

Not far from here in Bearsden lie the better-known remains of a Roman bathhouse. If you can, try and combine your visits.

Antonine Wall: the most northerly border of the Roman Empire

In the mid-2nd century the Antonine Wall was the most northerly border of the Roman Empire. For some reason it was abandoned just a few years after construction ended. The turf and wood structure eroded over the centuries (despite a brief reoccupation of the wall in the early 3rd century). As a result, it's harder to find remains of the Antonine Wall than the stone-built Hadrian's Wall in England, so many Scots are unaware of this engineering miracle. However, the route of the Antonine Wall crosses the north of Glasgow, in some places only around 8 km north of Central Station.

On a good day, you can drive from the centre of Glasgow and in around 25 minutes visit several remains of the Antonine Wall. From east to west, you can see remains at places such as Duntocher; Roman Park, Bearsden; Roman bath house, Bearsden; New

Kilpatrick Cemetery, Bearsden; Peel Park, Kirkintilloch; and Bar Hill fort. The route was originally punctuated by forts, fortlets, bathhouses and barracks, and today the remains range from stone foundations to ghostly impressions left on the tops of hills where the Romans constructed defensive forts that allowed them to control the local tribes. Many of the distance slabs and other artefacts left by Roman legionnaires and later found along the route of the wall can be seen at Glasgow's Hunterian Museum.

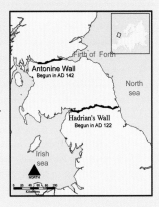

Visit antoninewall.org/map for information on all the sites along the route of the Antonine Wall.

CLYDEBANK MUSEUM

Clydebank's sewing-machine heritage

Clydebank Town Hall
5 Hall Street, Clydebank, G81 1UB
Monday–Saturday 10am–4.30pm
Clydebank train station

Above the entrance to Clydebank Town Hall is a weathered coat of arms that once belonged to this district. If you look carefully, you can see a tiny sewing machine. Below it is a ship. Both represent industries that once dominated this area. To find out more, do visit the small but fascinating Clydebank Museum inside the town hall.

Today Clydebank is a mere shadow of its former self. During Scotland's industrial heyday, Clydebank's ships and other products were sold throughout the world. Today the grandeur of the town hall seems at odds with the shabbier buildings nearby but try and imagine the year 1900 when a massive parade was held here to celebrate the laying of the

foundation stone. The parade included workers from the shipyards and the Singer sewing-machine factory.

The Singer story began in 1851, when an American named Isaac Merritt Singer created a domestic-use sewing machine that was revolutionary in its day – similar in impact to the introduction of the iPhone. Singer machines would later be sold around the world and Glasgow was chosen as the site of an international manufacturing base. The factory was founded in Kilbowie in Clydebank in the 1880s and dominated the skyline with a landmark 61-metre-high clock tower. It would become the largest sewing-machine factory in the world, employing 16,000 people by the 1960s.

Being a worker at the Singer factory meant being part of a unique community with recreational facilities, clubs and regular festivities. However, from the 1960s, competition from abroad made the factory too expensive to run and it closed in 1980. The building, including the famous clock tower, was demolished. Clydebank's shipbuilding firms were also in decline and the area would never be the same again. A new coat of arms produced in the 1970s still has a ship but the sewing machine has disappeared. However, inside the museum, you can see many wonderful examples of vintage Singer sewing machines.

The town hall was designed by James Miller, one of Glasgow's greatest architects. His plans incorporated a courtroom, police station, library, council chambers and baths. You can still see the old cells and baths today.

The museum also contains a memorial to the German bombing attack of 13–15 March 1941 that killed 528 people, injured over 600 others and destroyed thousands of homes. The impact on the local community was devastating – everyone knew at least one victim. The plaque inside the town hall lists the victims, a reminder of a tragic event of which many Glaswegians today are unaware.

Isaac Merritt Singer was a larger-than-life character. A child of German immigrants, he invented a machine to drill rock and used the money he made from the patent to fulfil his dream of becoming an actor. By chance he was asked to look at a sewing machine already on the market and spotted a way to improve the design. Within a few years he had set up his own company producing sewing machines for the mass market, a revolutionary development. He became a multimillionaire and created America's first truly global company. His personal life was complicated and scandalous. Singer fathered 24 children by several different wives and mistresses. One was a Parisian woman said to have been the model for the Statue of Liberty.

INCHINNAN PARISH CHURCH GRAVESTONES

Relics of a Celtic and a Templar past

Old Greenock Rd, Inchinnan, Renfrew, PA4 9PE
Open 24 hrs
Bus: 23

The Templar Stones at Inchinnan are among the most striking historical features in the Greater Glasgow area. In the 12th century the land around here, including the old parish church, was given by King David I to the legendary Knights Templar. When the latter were suppressed in the early 14th century, their lands were given to another religious-military order founded in the Holy Land during the time of the Crusades – the Knights of St John of Jerusalem. The Reformation in 1560 saw the lands then taken from the Knights of St John and passed through various aristocratic estates.

According to legend, the original parish church of All Hallows was founded by St Conval. The medieval building was demolished and rebuilt in later years, finally being pulled down to make way for the construction of Glasgow airport in the mid-1960s. The current church is therefore a modern replacement, but the Celtic and Templar Stones were brought here from the old site in 1965.

The three Celtic Stones date from the 9th to the 11th century, when this area was used as a burial place for royalty and aristocrats of the ancient Kingdom of Strathclyde. Inside their protective metal cage, the central stone is probably a shrine or sarcophagus cover. The Celtic carvings on the sandstone include animals and interlace patterns, similar in style to the Govan Stones found in Govan Parish Church.

To the rear of the church are ten gravestones known as the Templar Stones. Four (the ones with the sloping sides) may have marked the burial places of Knights Templar, bearing faint images of swords and other tools. In recent years, historians have taken digital photographs and analysed them to see details that are not visible to the naked eye, revealing hidden initials, dates and carved symbols including swords. The gravestones date from the 12th to the 17th century, although one (no. 7: bottom left on the information board) might be much older and may come from a similar period to the three Celtic Stones.

ST CONVAL'S STONE
AND THE ARGYLL STONE

Magical flying stone

Grounds of the Normandy Hotel
Inchinnan Rd, Renfrew, PA4 9EJ
Buses: Clydeflyer 901, 906

Tucked away in the grounds of the Normandy Hotel – less than 11 km from central Glasgow – is a fenced-off plot with two stones, rarely visited and looking rather neglected. One is called St Conval's Stone (also known as St Conval's Chariot), the other the Argyll Stone.

The story of St Conval's Stone is the more extraordinary: St Conval was a follower of St Kentigern, better known as St Mungo – the founder and patron saint of Glasgow. The son of an Irish chieftain, Conval was born in Ireland around AD 570. According to legend, he was standing on the Irish coast praying to God and asking him how to lead his life. As he did so, the stone he was standing on broke away from the earth and flew with St Conval across the Irish Sea to Inchinnan. He founded a church here and began work as a missionary among the pagan Picts. St Conval died around AD 630 and is thought to have been buried in Inchinnan.

The stone later formed the base of a Christian cross. Pilgrims would come to drink the water that flowed through a hollow in the stone, believing it possessed miraculous healing properties.

The Argyle Stone is so called as the Earl of Argyle (1629–85) was resting by it when he was captured by his opponents in 1685 after leading an uprising against King James II. Argyle had a dramatic life, on one occasion escaping imprisonment from Edinburgh Castle after dressing as a woman. His rebel army of 1685 failed to win widespread support, however, and he ended up at this stone in Inchinnan with just one supporter, all his other men having fled for their lives.

It is said that when local men tried to capture him, he tried to fire his pistol but the gunpowder was damp and he was struck on the head by a weaver. He was later brought to Edinburgh where he was executed on the Scottish version of the guillotine, known as the Maiden. Argyle's father had suffered the same fate years before.

LUMA TOWER

An art deco gem

Linthouse, 510 Shieldhall Road, G51 4HE
Govan Subway station

Stranded near the M8 and the busy Shieldhall Road, the elegant 25-metre-high Luma Tower seems a long way from Stockholm. Still, this architectural gem has an unusual connection with Sweden and a largely forgotten period of Glasgow's history.

Part of a light-bulb factory built in 1938, the tower was designed in a late-period art deco style by Cornelius Armour for the British Luma Co-operative Electric Lamp Society Ltd. It was in the tower that light bulbs were tested.

The connection between Glasgow and Luma, a district of Stockholm, has its origins in the co-operative movement that emerged during the Industrial Revolution. The harshness of working conditions for many people in the new factories encouraged new groups to create alternative ways of running a business – the co-operative organisation. 'Co-ops' produced goods and services that were affordable for customers and members, and not solely designed to maximise profits.

Scotland was at the forefront of the co-operative revolution: in 1868 the Scottish Co-operative Wholesale Society (SCWS) was founded. At a factory in Shieldhall, it manufactured goods such as furniture and footwear, all sold by other co-operative societies.

In 1930 a Swedish co-operative society built a light bulb factory in Luma, near Stockholm, the design very similar to this Glasgow building. This same Swedish co-op joined forces in the late 1930s with the SCWS to create the British Luma Co-operative Electric Lamp Society Ltd in Shieldhall.

The collaboration between the Swedish and Glasgow co-operatives resulted from a desire to take on a secret international cartel formed by the leading manufacturers of light bulbs. This cartel, described as the 'Great Light Bulb Conspiracy', wanted to stifle innovation in light-bulb design so that consumers had to buy more of their products. In contrast, the Swedish and Scottish co-ops developed their own longer-lasting light bulbs to benefit ordinary people. It was a brave move: imagine a worker-led business trying to compete with Apple or Samsung today! However, for many years the co-ops made a real difference to working people's lives.

Light bulbs continued to be made at this site until the 1960s, and the SCWS later merged with an English co-operative organisation. After years of uncertainty and threatened demolition, the Luma building was saved and converted for residential use, reopening in 1996.

Memories of the workhouse: a relic of the city's grim past

Standing outside a forbidding-looking building on the east side of the Southern General Hospital in Govan is as close as you can get to the city's grim connections with the workhouses of the 19th and early 20th centuries. Only visible from the outside, the original Govan Union Workhouse was built here in the 1870s. After it closed in the 1920s, much of the structure was incorporated into the new hospital complex.

The male and female wings of the workhouse (or 'poor house') stood on either side of the entrance. The workhouse could hold several hundred inmates, including the destitute, those needing medical treatment and the mentally ill.

The 1881 census gives a snapshot of those unfortunate enough to end up here. Many were simply too old to look after themselves, but others were much younger and included housewives, commercial travellers, scholars, blacksmiths and shoemakers.

The Govan Workhouse was built during the heyday of Britain's workhouse programme in the late 19th century. These grim

institutions were deliberately meant to be places of last resort, with such unwelcoming conditions that inmates would be discouraged from staying any longer than absolutely necessary. The food provided was inadequate and inmates were required to perform back-breaking, repetitive tasks that often had no purpose. Inmates frequently became ill, making it even harder for them to escape.

The brutality of workhouses is immortalised in Charles Dickens' *Oliver Twist* – he and others encouraged a public debate about how the poor could be better treated. In the late 19th century campaigners for social change and progressive politicians began to push for reforms that would provide a basic welfare safety net for ordinary people.

Workhouses started to close down in the early 20th century as the poor had greater access to unemployment benefits and state pensions. Many were demolished, while some – like the one in Govan – had their structures incorporated into the new hospitals then being built.

Since then, nearly all the other workhouse buildings in Glasgow have disappeared – the sole exception being this relic of the city's grim past in Govan.

HORATIO'S GARDEN

Inspiring secret garden within the Spinal Injuries Unit

The Queen Elizabeth National Spinal Injuries Unit
Queen Elizabeth University Hospital – 1345 Govan Rd, G51 4TF
To arrange a group tour, contact Lucy Shergold, Tour Co-ordinator,
on lucyS@horatiosgarden.org.uk or call 07859 940769 for more information
Cardonald train station
Bus: 77 Hospital Connect

Not many Glaswegians visit the National Spinal Injuries Unit at the Queen Elizabeth University Hospital. However, it is home to a special place – Horatio's Garden – which is open to the public by appointment.

Opened in 2016, the garden has turned a previously dull part of the hospital into an inspiring place for patients at Scotland's Spinal Injuries Unit. Patients can spend time here, away from the wards, and meet friends and relatives. The garden has also transformed the outlook for patients whose injuries make it difficult to leave the unit.

This well-kept secret is divided into several distinct spaces, each contributing to the overall impression. At its heart is the courtyard garden, brimming with colour and life; it features a large, calming water feature. Dahlias, anemone and verbena are just some of the beautiful plants that welcome patients and visitors all year round. The woodland walk features immersive planning that changes with the seasons and is a haven for wildlife. There are also sheltered spots that allow visitors some respite from Glasgow's unpredictable weather.

The garden was created by the well-known designer James Alexander-Sinclair. It is named after an extraordinary young man, Horatio Chapple, who died – aged just 17 – during an attack by a polar bear on an expedition party camping in a remote area of Norway in 2011. Horatio had planned to study medicine and had volunteered at the Salisbury Spinal Treatment Centre during his school holidays, researching the creation of a garden there.

After Horatio's death his parents – both in the medical profession – were inspired to set up a charity named Horatio's Garden, which hopes to create similar green spaces at half a dozen spinal injury units up and down Britain, including London, Stoke Mandeville and Cardiff.

The garden welcomes visitors and also new volunteers to help maintain it. If you are interested in either opportunity, see the contact details opposite.

CROOKSTON CASTLE

Glasgow's only surviving medieval castle, hidden away in the unlikeliest of spots

170 Brockburn Road, G53 5RY
0141 883 9606
historicenvironment.scot/visit-a-place/places/crookston-castle
1 April–30 September: daily 9.30am–5.30pm
1 October–31 March: Saturday–Wednesday 10am–4pm
Free
X8 bus service (Pollok and Crookston Castle circular) from Glasgow city centre

Glasgow's lack of major castles may cost it dearly when squaring up to other tourism-driven cities like Edinburgh or Stirling, but did you know that there is one within the city limits, still standing and yet hidden away in the unlikeliest of spots?

Of course, the Bishop's Castle which once stood in the medieval heart of the city centre is long gone: all that remains of the grand building once neighbour to Glasgow Cathedral is the name, Castle Street. But head south to the neighbourhood of Pollok and you'll find once fortified, now ruined stone walls sitting on a hilltop as imposing as any of Scotland's celebrated castles. Crookston is Glasgow's only surviving medieval castle, built in the 1400s but with foundations dating back to the 1100s.

Historians see Crookston as an anomaly because its layout is almost unique in Scotland: a high central tower surrounded by four square corner towers, although only one of those (in the north-east) remains intact.

Today, the building is maintained by Historic Scotland and can be visited during daytime opening hours. The hillside spot is surrounded by unassuming modern housing – and while people living nearby are no doubt proud of their towering neighbour, few elsewhere in Glasgow know much about Crookston Castle or its links to key figures in Scottish history.

The structure is thought to have been built by Sir Alexander Stewart, lord of Crookston, in the early 1400s. The Stewarts later became earls of Lennox, including Henry Stuart, Lord Darnley, who would go on to marry his first cousin, the famous Mary Queen of Scots, and father James VI of Scotland, later James I of England.

Granted, every castle in Scotland claims a link with the ill-fated queen, but the noble family who once ruled this small rural area in the south of Glasgow, and their famous descendants, make Crookston Castle a far more interesting place than meets the eye.

Fast forward to more recent history and the castle has another key role to play in Glasgow's story: it was used as an aircraft watch tower during the Second World War and the infamous Clydebank Blitz.

Nowadays, visitors climb the hill for unrivalled views over the south-east of Glasgow and enjoy wandering over the sturdy stone walls.

GLASGOW MUSEUM RESOURCE CENTRE

The greatest treasure house in Glasgow

200 Woodhead Road, G53 7NN
0141 276 9300
GMCRbookings@glasgowlife.org.uk
GMCRbookings@glasgowlife.org.uk for information on tours
Organised tours only, upon prior appointment
Daily 10am–5pm (11am on Fri & Sun)
Nitshill train station

Well off the tourist path, the Glasgow Museum Resource Centre (GMRC) is one of the most fascinating places in Glasgow as this is where the city stores all its museum-quality objects while they're not on display in the main museums. The public can't just walk around this vast complex like an ordinary museum, but there are organised tours that allow visitors to sample some of the treasures held here.

The collection is organised into categories: Natural History, Technology, World Cultures, Arms and Armour, and Art and Painting.

On the hour-long tour you might see a painting by Titian, a portrait of Billy Connolly by John Byrne, intricately carved doorways from India, furniture designed by Charles Rennie Mackintosh or an Eskimo's canoe.

The range of what's on offer is extraordinary and the tour guides provide a valuable insight into objects that might on the surface look ordinary but have a fascinating story to tell.

The GMRC is needed because Glasgow's main museums can only put on display a fraction (around 2%) of all the objects the city owns. The rest (around 1.4 million objects) are largely held at the GMRC in 17 enormous storage 'pods'. This is where paintings are restored, and curators select objects to be moved to one of the main museums as collections are rotated.

While most of the objects are held securely in cabinets, the GMRC puts on regular tours for the public. Some are 'drop-in' tours that take an hour and show a range of items of interest, others have specific themes. To avoid disappointment, it's best to contact the GMRC to find out what tours are available.

ARTHURLIE CROSS

King Arthur's gravestone?

Springhill Road, Barrhead, G78 2BB
Barrhead train station

Located just 13 km from central Glasgow, the Arthurlie Cross stands behind a railing by a small road in Barrhead. Measuring just over 2 metres and bearing Celtic interlace carved panels, this sandstone pillar is believed to date back to the 10th or 11th century. However, local legend also links it to the mythical King Arthur, even suggesting it once served as his gravestone.

The stone has been moved about over the years, most recently from nearby Arthurlie House. It has also been used as part of a bridge and in a gatepost, but at least is now protected behind a railing.

Most Glaswegians are unaware that Scotland has strong connections to the legend of King Arthur. Some have speculated that the legend was based on the 6th-century Scottish figure Arthur Mac Aedan, who was born in Stirling and lived in Argyll.

Author Adam Ardrey argues this in his book, *Finding Arthur*, believing that the legendary hero came from Scotland. Ardrey also believes that Argyll may have been the location of the fabled Camelot. Mac Aedan led an army that defeated invaders in the late 6th century and he was buried on the island of Iona.

Much of the speculation about the Scottish Arthur is based on the work of Nennius, a Welsh monk who wrote *The History of the Britons* in around 830. It has an account of Arthur and the 12 battles he took part in and historians have long sought to match Nennius' descriptions of the landscape of each battle to modern-day locations. It has been suggested that in one of these battles Arthur defeated the outlawed sons of Caw in the vicinity of what is today Cambuslang. Other battles are described in ways that do suggest the possibility they took place in Scotland.

THE SECRET WATERFALL
OF ROUKEN GLEN PARK

⑪

A waterfall hidden for centuries from public view

Rouken Glen Road, G46 7UG
0141 638 7411
roukenglenpark.co.uk
Whitecraigs train station
Buses: 38, 38A, 38C

Glasgow may be known as the 'Dear Green Place' (from the Gaelic *Glaschu*) and its public parks are plentiful – but few cities can claim to have a waterfall that's been hidden for centuries from public view.

Rouken Glen Park has existed in some form since 1530 and has subsequently been the site of a nature-led textile factory and a leisure facility for rich Victorians escaping the city.

The long-gone Birkenshaw Cottage was even a holiday-home destination visited by the city's infamous murderess, Madeleine Smith, who was brought to trial for the murder of her lover, Pierre Emile L'Angelier, in 1857 – just one long-surviving legend associated with Rouken Glen.

First records of the area show that the land (then known as Birkenshaw) was gifted by James V to the 1st Earl of Montgomery. It passed through numerous hands, including the Crum family of Thornliebank, who expanded the printworks established in the late 1700s as well as much of the park landscaping still visible today.

The place was gifted to the people of Glasgow in 1906 and is now in the hands of the local authority in East Renfrewshire. Today it's a well-trodden spot for families and dog walkers. It regularly scoops awards, and in 2016 won the Fields in Trust "Best UK Park" award.

Still, there remain hidden depths to Rouken Glen.

The main waterfall provides a centrepiece but in 2016 a second, artificial water feature was rediscovered during restoration works in a previously closed-off area of the park.

The area known as Lovers Walk now has a boardwalk pathway which is open to the public, exposing iron beams and wooden boards where Newfield Printworks stood some 200 years ago.

ROUND TOLL

A historic toll building

1 Barrhead Road, G43 1AD
Junction of Pollockshaws Road and Nether Auldhouse Road
Pollockshaws West train station

Marooned on a busy roundabout by Pollockshaws stands an isolated small building known as the Round Toll. It is old, but no one is certain exactly when it was built, some suggesting a date as early as the 1750s, others claiming as late as 1820. What is certain, however, is that for many decades this was where a toll collector worked, stopping passing travellers to extract a toll – or fee – for using the neighbouring roads.

Road tolls began to be collected in this area in the 1750s and at one time there were about six different toll collection points in and around Pollockshaws. People would make bids to the local authorities to become a toll keeper, paying a fixed fee in return for the privilege of taxing passers-by. Much of the traffic that passed by the Round Toll was rural in nature: cattle drovers and farm workers moving between farms in Ayrshire and the big markets in Glasgow.

The once famous Pollockshaws annual fair also attracted many visitors. Eventually an enterprising toll keeper obtained a licence to sell alcohol so the Round Toll could extract even more cash from thirsty travellers.

In the days before the state took responsibility for maintaining public roads, tolls like this were common throughout the Glasgow area. It made short journeys very expensive for people caught each time at toll offices that were often not that far apart.

The Round Toll is also a rare reminder of the day when Pollockshaws was still an independent burgh whose inhabitants had a reputation for being quite quirky. It only merged with Glasgow in 1912 and today just feels like another suburb of a big city.

The collection of tolls continued up until the 1880s, after which this unusual building, with its conical slate roof and chimney, was used for a variety of purposes including a carriage hire shop, a pub and – right up until 1963 – a residential dwelling.

In more recent years, it has been used as a store house by the council. As new roads were laid during the 20th century, the Round Toll became increasingly isolated. It now stands unloved and largely ignored on the modern roundabout you see today.

JOHN MACLEAN MEMORIAL

Memories of a Glasgow radical – the Russian Bolsheviks' consul in Scotland

Pollockshaws, G43 1RY
Between Riverford Road and Greenview Street in front of the Old Town House
Pollockshaws West train station

Near the Old Town House in Pollockshaws is a modest memorial to one of the most controversial and radical characters in the city's recent history – John Maclean. Born in Pollockshaws in 1879, he only lived to the age of 44, but at his death thousands of ordinary Glaswegians turned out to remember him.

Maclean (1879–1923) grew up in modest circumstances, his father dying when John was young. Maclean become a teacher and then got involved in groups linked to socialism and Marxism. His opposition to the First World War saw him imprisoned by the authorities. It cost him his job and he became even more radical, espousing a Marxist view of how the nation needed to change.

Charismatic, he appealed to a mass of radical-leaning, working-class people in Glasgow, this being the era of 'Red Clydeside'. The authorities considered him 'the most dangerous figure in Britain' and feared he would encourage people to undermine the war effort. Maclean was also noticed further afield – he gained the respect of Trotsky and Lenin and was appointed the Russian Bolsheviks' consul in Scotland.

Maclean was prosecuted for sedition in 1918 and imprisoned, his passionate defence making him an even greater legend among the city's left-leaning groups. It is said that around 250,000 Glaswegians turned out to celebrate his release in 1918 – an astonishing sign of his popularity, which explains why the British government found him such a threat.

However, the five separate periods he spent in prison impacted his health and he was subjected to force-feeding. In the remainder of his life, he tried to become Labour MP for the Gorbals and founded a communist party. Poor and suffering from pneumonia, Maclean died after falling ill while giving a speech in 1923. A few days before he died, with typical generosity, he apparently gave his only overcoat to a destitute man he had met by chance.

While he has many enemies both inside the radical left and elsewhere, Maclean had a major impact in Glasgow and 20,000 mourners followed his funeral procession. Today, however, he is a largely unknown figure to many Glaswegians and this memorial is one of the few reminders of the city's most extraordinary citizen of recent times.

MARY QUEEN OF SCOTS MEMORIAL

When a queen saw her army destroyed

North-east side of Old Castle Road
Court Knowe, Cathcart, G44 5DT
Cathcart train station

The Battle of Langside on 13 May 1568 changed British history for ever. On that day, just before 10 o'clock in the morning, Mary Queen of Scots watched from this hill as her force of around 6,000 men far below fought an army under the command of her bitter enemy and half-brother, James Stuart, 1st Earl of Moray. Mary was soon in despair, realising her army was being routed.

A memorial was first erected here in 1799 to mark the spot from where she is believed to have watched the carnage but it was removed by the Glasgow Corporation in 1927 and is now kept by Glasgow Museums. The modern replacement is little known even to locals who use the park.

By the day of the battle, Mary was already a tragic figure. Still in her 20s, she had been Queen of both France and Scotland and had a strong claim to the English throne of her cousin, Elizabeth I. However, everything had gone wrong in her life. When her first husband, the King of France, died, she returned to Scotland – a country she hardly knew. As Queen of the Scots, she was overwhelmed by the sectarian, aristocratic power politics that dominated the country in the 16th century. She was eventually imprisoned by her enemies and forced to abdicate in favour of her infant son, James (James VI of Scotland, later James I of England).

Mary escaped her prison in Lochleven Castle and gathered a small army, hoping to regain power in Scotland. However, when she and her troops were passing through nearby Langside on their way to seek refuge at Dumbarton Castle, they were ambushed by Moray (acting as Regent for her infant son James) at the head of his own army.

The battle was over in an hour, leaving Moray the victor. Mary's hopes of recovering her throne were dashed and she fled south, seeking protection from Elizabeth I. It was an unfortunate decision as she was regarded as a dangerous rival and executed in 1587. Ironically, Mary's son James would succeed Elizabeth to the English throne in 1603.

What if Mary had won here instead? She might have recovered her throne and succeeded Elizabeth in England, changing the course of British history.

Those interested in this era of history should visit the much better known Battle of Langside monument just south of Queen's Park – close to where the fighting took place. It was designed by the Victorian architect Alexander Skirving and erected in 1887 to mark the 300th anniversary of Mary's death. It was said to have been a labour of love for which Skirving declined a fee. A time capsule containing coins, newspapers and a copy of Sir Walter Scott's book *The Abbot* (which refers to the battle) was buried underneath.

Glasgow - To the North and East

WALLACE'S WELL

Final drink for a Scottish legend

Langmuirhead Road, near Robroyston, G33 1PP
Buses: 57, 57A

Beside a quiet road leading into countryside near Roybroyston is a small opening in a stone wall beside a stream. This is Wallace's Well – by tradition the spring was used by William Wallace (1270-1305) when he was in the area.

If true, it is most likely where he gulped down some water on his last day as a free man. Wallace would not recognise the structure you see today: it has been restored in recent years and lies beside a new housing estate. It was at risk of being demolished due to housing development, but pressure from historians, the media and organisations such as the Clan Wallace Society saved Wallace's Well. The earliest mention of the well is in an epic poem by the Scots bard Blind Harry in the 15th century, long after Wallace died.

No one can be certain that Wallace did drink from this spring. This is hardly surprising as not a great deal is known about Wallace as a person, despite the fact that he became famous around the world thanks to Mel Gibson's portrayal of the Scottish hero in the 1995 film *Braveheart*. Wallace may have been a humble mercenary, and by one account, was tall and solidly built, but his anonymous existence changed in the 1290s. Edward I of England began to apply pressure on the Scottish nobility, wanting to be accepted as their monarch, and his army subsequently invaded Scotland.

From nowhere, Wallace became one of the key military leaders of the Scottish resistance. His determination and tactical skills led to some impressive victories against the English, most notably the Battle of Stirling Bridge in 1297. Wallace was knighted soon after, but in the following years, while he stayed true to the cause of Scottish Independence, the aristocracy of his own country began to wilt under pressure and switch their allegiance to Edward I.

By 1304 Wallace was an outlaw and fugitive, possibly spending time in Europe to seek support from the French and others. In August 1305, he was commonly thought to have come to this area, then known as Rab Rae's Toun, to hide in a cottage or barn a few hundred yards from here. On 5 August, he was captured by a Scottish nobleman named Sir John Menteith. It is believed that Wallace's close friend, Kerlie, was killed near the well.

Wallace was sent down to London to be tried, although the result was a foregone conclusion. On or around 23 August, aged just 35, he was executed in front of thousands of Londoners. The contrast between his brutal death and his time in this quiet spot is hard to imagine. In London he was dragged through the streets, hanged until nearly dead, had his genitals cut off, and then his guts were pulled out of his body and burnt. He was finally beheaded, and his body cut into pieces.

There is a Wallace Monument very near here on the site believed to have been where he was captured (on Lumloch Road), so make sure to visit this as well if you are in Robroyston.

POSSIBLE RENNIE MACKINTOSH HOUSES

A family affair?

140–142 Balgrayhill Road, G21 3TN
Springburn train station
Buses: 57, 87, 88

On Balgrayhill Road in Springburn are a couple of red sandstone semi-detached houses that seem fairly ordinary. You wouldn't give them a second glance unless you were aware they *might* have been designed by Charles Rennie Mackintosh (1868–1928), Scotland's most celebrated architect.

The address rarely features on the increasingly popular Mackintosh building tours and admittedly bears none of the distinctive features usually associated with him. However, Thomas Howarth, in his 1952

book about the architect, formally suggested that the buildings were early works by Mackintosh and speculation as to their true origins has continued ever since.

While no clear documentary evidence exists of Mackintosh's involvement, it is known that the houses were built for his cousin James Hamilton, who moved into one in 1890 and rented out the other. The houses were then known as Redclyffe and Torrisdale, and it seems that Howarth picked up on a Hamilton family tradition still circulating in the mid-20th century that Mackintosh was involved in the design.

At the time the houses were built, Mackintosh was only 22 and still establishing his reputation, so it is understandable that he was not yet demonstrating the confident style for which he would become famous later on. Despite lingering doubts about his involvement, the possibility was enough to ensure the houses were saved from demolition in the 1960s, a fate that neighbouring houses were not lucky enough to escape.

SPRINGBURN WINTER GARDENS ③

A remnant of its former glory

Springburn Park, G21 3AY
facebook.com/springburnwintergardens
First Bus 88 (to Balgrayhill Road)

Once a major draw to the district of Springburn, you might walk by the Winter Gardens today without giving them a second look. The

shell of the once grand glasshouse is half-heartedly fenced off although urban explorers have no problem sneaking inside. Its former glory is at once obvious and saddening: what a shame that landmarks like this can fall into such disrepair! Of course, there are locals working to change it all, and one day Springburn Winter Gardens may be restored. In the meantime, what seems important is to preserve a once-celebrated gem in the north of Glasgow.

The 55-metre-long glasshouse was built in 1899 as a condition of Glasgow Corporation's accepting a £12,000 gift from Hugh Reid, of the North British Locomotive Company, to finance the construction of the nearby Springburn Public Halls.

With locomotive manufacturing playing such a vital role in the community of Springburn, it's little wonder that the Winter Gardens were beloved by subsequent generations – the A-listed structure, with all its greenery and grandeur, must have seemed a world away from the industrial boom outside the park. From exotic plants to regular exhibitions and events beneath the glass-domed ceiling, it's not hard to imagine this oasis from the smog of the booming city beyond.

It was once the largest glasshouse in Scotland but by the latter half of the 20th century it had fallen into disrepair, with Glasgow District Council forced to close it rather than meet the restoration costs. The building was listed in May 1985, two days before the council was due to consider an application to demolish Springburn Winter Gardens. As a result, the shell of the building still stands today ... but it has a long way to go before visitors will pass through its doors again.

The glasshouse was put on the market in the 1980s but failed to attract any interest, falling prey instead to vandalism and continued decay. Plans to restore it to its former glory fell flat again in 2004, when the estimated cost of repairs was a whopping £7–£8 million.

After years of stalled plans, the Springburn Winter Gardens Trust was formed in 2014 in the hope of bringing the building back into community use. Emergency repairs to the steelwork were carried out in 2017 and the structure is now stable, although its overgrown appearance and lack of windows leave it a far cry from its starting point over a century ago.

Work remains ongoing, thanks to the efforts of the community group, and Springburn Winter Gardens stands as one of many examples of Glasgow neighbourhoods banding together to save local landmarks.

Their work is only viable if people continue to visit the place and so, shell or not, fenced off or otherwise, it seems more important than ever to hop on a bus to Springburn and view the Winter Gardens – to see the once-loved building as it is now, and to imagine what it could mean to Glasgow in the future.

BALGRAY TOWER

A hidden castle in the heart of Springburn

52 Broomfield Road, Springburn, G21 3UB
Private property: no entry
McGills 72 bus (to Balgrayhill Road)

From the long-demolished Bishop's Castle by Glasgow Cathedral to the ruins of Crookston Castle in the south, there were more fortified walls in the city than you might think. Still, few people would look to the north of Glasgow, and the post-industrial, largely residential area of Springburn, for Gothic turrets. Granted, this is pure Gothic revival, built around 1820 by a wealthy tea merchant, but Balgray Tower, a private residence on Broomfield Road, certainly attracts the eye.

People often ask what the castellated tower they can see peeking up in Springburn really is. The answer is: a very unusual home, first owned by a tea merchant called Captain Breeze, who named it Breeze's Tower (no points for originality there). There's little information about him although British Listed Buildings give the first owner as a Duncan of Mosesfield, so perhaps Captain Breeze was more of a nickname.

Springburn is known for its heavy industry, particularly the manufacturing of railway locomotives. The former headquarters of the North British Locomotive Company and four of its main sites were once located in the north of the city.

Balgray Tower predates all those developments, leaving you to wonder just how different Springburn was at the time that it was built … and how much the view from the top has changed since.

The stone villa fell into ruin for a time as housing schemes grew up around it, but the B-listed building has since been restored and now boasts the original 18-metre-high tower, accessible via a spiral staircase and offering 360-degree citywide views over the ramparts. Below lie five bedrooms, a huge lounge and an equally large kitchen as well as private gardens. The place has a current estimated value of £230,000 according to the last home report, which isn't bad for your very own castle – it's safe to assume that the price will continue to rise even if house prices stagnate elsewhere in Springburn.

Unfortunately, there's a large wall surrounding the property so it's not possible to get close to it, let alone climb to the top of the tower. Still, there are prime spots to view it: stand below on Carleston Street and you'll see the turret poking up between tenements and 20th-century builds.

Ghost stories

There are many stories surrounding the spot, as you'd expect from any Gothic turret standing out among rows of council houses. Ghost stories associated with 52 Broomfield Road include a maid who died in the tower and a lady in green carrying a small dog.

BAS-RELIEF OF A LOCOMOTIVE ⑤

In its heyday, Springburn produced a quarter of all the world's railway locomotives

Former Headquarters of the North British Locomotive Company
120–136 Flemington Street, G21 4BF
Springburn train station

At the entrance to the grand building at 120–136 Flemington Street, a surprising bas-relief of a steam locomotive adorns the façade. Although nothing on this quiet street suggests any connection with the railways, in its heyday a number of major firms in Springburn produced around a quarter of all the railway locomotives in the world.

Constructed in 1908, the building was the headquarters of the once mighty North British Locomotive Company (NBL), then a recently formed company that incorporated several much older local manufacturers.

Its architect, James Miller, was known particularly for his work on railway stations. At the time, the NBL employed 8,000 people, principally at its Atlas and Hyde Park works in Springburn. Around 400 locomotives were built in Springburn each year, making the NBL the largest manufacturer of its kind in Europe and the British Empire.

Many of the locomotives built in Springburn were transported by road to the Clyde, where they were shipped to destinations around the world, including key markets in the British Empire. Often public processions would accompany the biggest locomotives as they were hauled through the streets down to the river, where huge cranes would load them onto ships ready for export. India alone took delivery of over 6,000 NBL engines.

By the time the Flemington Street HQ was built, Springburn had been a centre for locomotive manufacturing since the 1860s. It was a natural choice as railway lines passed through bringing coal to the city and supplying the nearby St Rollox chemical works.

In the second half of the 20th century, locomotive manufacturing in Springburn started to decline. The dissolving British Empire was no longer such a captive market, while the NBL struggled to navigate the change from steam locomotives to those powered by diesel and electricity. The company finally closed in 1962, having produced the huge total of 28,000 locomotives.

The NBL's old manufacturing sites were later cleared for use as industrial estates and educational facilities. This run-down, yet still grand building is a rare legacy of the golden age of locomotive manufacture in Springburn.

THE GROOVE MARKS
OF MONKLAND CANAL

A relic of Glasgow's lost canal

Pedestrian subway under Castle Street at Royston Road, G21 2QU
Visible at Summerlee Heritage Park (Coatbridge, ML5 1QD: daily, 10am–4pm)
or Drumpellier Park (Coatbridge, ML5 2EH: daily, 10.30am–7.30pm)

Groove marks on a wall in a dark subway under Castle Street are a ghostly reminder of the Monkland Canal that used to stretch from Calderbank, near Airdrie, right into the heart of Glasgow at Townhead Basin. The marks were made by the ropes used by horses pulling barges along the canal.

The construction of the Monkland Canal was one of many Scottish engineering triumphs during the Industrial Revolution, though sadly much of the route has long been filled in, most now lying directly under the M8 motorway. However, remaining sections can still be seen in odd places like this subway, and in the Coatbridge area at Summerlee Heritage Park and Drumpellier Park.

Construction began in 1771 and the canal eventually ran for some 19 km. The purpose was to reduce the cost of transporting coal into Glasgow by bringing it in from the coalfields of Monkland. It was later connected by the 'cut of the junction' to the much larger Forth and Clyde Canal, which ran across the middle of Scotland.

Engineer James Watt, whose improvements to the steam engine were arguably the single most important contribution to the Industrial Revolution, supervised the initial construction of the canal although his involvement was short-lived. For years, construction was blighted by lack of funds and it took a quarter of a century to complete.

Those who backed the original plan could not have foreseen the railway revolution that occurred during the 19th century and which impacted many canal routes.

Despite competition from the new railways, the Monkland was still the most profitable canal in Scotland by 1837 – much of this was due to the development of ironworks in Coatbridge that created a huge demand not only for coal, but also for a means to transport iron ore and pig iron cheaply.

The golden era for the Monkland Canal was in the mid-19th century, when over 1 million tonnes of coal a year were moved along the water. It was later taken over by the Forth & Clyde Canal Company before being sold on to the Caledonian Railway Company. The latter was primarily concerned with investing in its railway and the Monkland Canal grew increasingly irrelevant as other forms of transport became cheaper and quicker.

The canal finally closed in the mid-20th century and during the 1960s most of it was filled in. This provided a convenient route for the M8 motorway to be built on. As a result, there are only a few remaining sections of Glasgow's 'lost' canal, the most substantial remains being visible in Summerlee and Drumpellier parks.

DENNISTOUN MILESTONE SCULPTURE

⑦

A forgotten time capsule

Duke Street (opp. junction with Annbank Street), G31 1QZ
Bellgrove train station

Every day, locals stand at the bus stop by the *Dennistoun Milestone* and fail to notice this strange sculpture that has been likened to Darth Vader. Commissioned by Dennistoun Community Council to celebrate the city's status as 1990 European City of Culture, the monument was created by Jim Buckley (b. 1957), a prominent sculptor from Cork who spent many years working and living in Scotland, including lecturing at the Glasgow School of Art and founding the Glasgow Sculpture Studios.

In Buckley's own words, 'The *Milestone* is intended to be a marker. The scale is small and intimate so as to function as an indicator of a "sense of place" – and to be a shrine or time capsule of the past and a monument to the future.' Its unusual abstract features were inspired by the design of a typical Glasgow tenement with its stair turrets and windows. Inside, Buckley placed a time capsule with local objects of interest and a written account of tenement life.

Buckley's sculpture was one of seven intended 'Glasgow Milestones' planned for the city as European City of Culture. The Dennistoun version was unveiled by the Lord Provost of Glasgow in September 1991. It remains one of the city's most unusual yet little-known pieces of public art.

BUFFALO BILL STATUE

Glasgow's cowboy past

63–87 Whitehill Street, G31 2LR
Belgrove train station

Hidden away in Dennistoun, looking out of place in front of a modern residential development, a statue of Colonel William F. Cody shows him riding a bucking bronco. But why would Glaswegians wish to remember Cody, better known as 'Buffalo Bill'?

Cody lived an extraordinary life: as a boy he worked on a wagon train before riding for the Pony Express and later served in the US army as a scout during the Indian Wars. As the myth of the Wild West began to be created in the media, Cody became its darling and for many around the world he epitomised the Western hero.

Cody cashed in on his fame, founding an American Wild West show that toured the world for many years. In late 1891 the show arrived in Glasgow – then one of the most industrialised cities in the world, and about as far away from the open plains of the American West as you could imagine. For three months, Cody's show packed out a 7,000-seater arena, created out of the recently vacated East End Exhibition Buildings in Dennistoun – near where the statue is located.

But it wasn't just a show. It involved real 'American Indians' who a few months before had been fighting the US cavalry and had been sent to Cody in order to 'pacify' them. Other performers included sharpshooter Annie Oakley, who went on to inspire *Annie Get Your Gun*. Cody's tour of Glasgow was full of drama both inside and outside the arena. He made a famous visit to Ibrox stadium when Rangers were playing and one of the Native Americans ended up in Barlinnie prison after getting drunk in an east end pub and hitting the show's promoter.

The visit had a big impact in Glasgow and was never forgotten, particularly by the children who grew up with stories of the Wild West and now bumped into real Native Americans strolling around the cold streets of the city's east end.

Although the myth of the Wild West does not have the same hold over today's Glaswegians as over those who flocked to Dennistoun in the 1890s, the legacy of Buffalo Bill can still be seen in the many Glaswegians who dress up in Western outfits at the city's Country & Western clubs. This statue is therefore a rare reminder of when the Wild West came to the east end.

FRANCIS KELLY'S GRAVE

A Glasgow hero for the US Navy

Sandymount Cemetery, 169 Croftspar Grove, G32 0JN
Shettleston train station (then 15-min. walk)

FRANCIS
KELLY

MEDAL OF HONOR
CMM
USS MERRIMAC
SP-AM WAR
JUL 5 1859
MAY 19 1938
AKA ARCHIBALD
HOUSTON

Archibald Houston was born in Anderston in Glasgow in 1859. Like many other Scots, he later moved to the United States and ended up joining the US Navy, changing his name to Francis Kelly. He wasn't obvious hero material, working as a modest stoker down in the boiler room that powered the steam engine of his ship, the USS *Merrimac*. However, fate had other plans for Francis Kelly.

In June 1898 the *Merrimac* took part in the Spanish-American War. Rear Admiral William T. Sampson ordered the ship to be sunk in order to block Santiago harbour in Cuba, the plan being to trap the Spanish fleet there. He asked for volunteers and Kelly was one of eight men who bravely stood forward.

The men sailed the ship towards the harbour but intense Spanish shelling destroyed the *Merrimac*'s steering gear. A sitting duck, the ship was then sunk by more Spanish artillery shells and torpedoes – the only American ship to suffer such a fate during the war.

Kelly and the seven other volunteers were lucky to escape with their lives but were captured by the Spanish and held as prisoners of war. Kelly was later released and his extraordinary bravery was recognised by the award of the Medal of Honor – the highest military award in the United States, the equivalent of the British Victoria Cross.

Kelly's official Medal of Honor citation reads: 'In connection with the sinking of the USS *Merrimac* at the entrance to the harbor of Santiago de Cuba, June 2, 1898. Despite heavy fire from the Spanish batteries, KELLY displayed extraordinary heroism throughout this operation.'

Kelly – the Glaswegian hero – remained in the navy after the war and later returned to his home city. Little more is known about him but he must have had some extraordinary stories to tell his old friends back home. He died aged 77 in 1938 and was largely forgotten, his gravestone overgrown with weeds.

In recent years, however, Kelly's achievement has been recognised again, culminating in 2017 when veterans of the Airborne Forces Association Scotland cleaned up his burial spot and commissioned a new cross and plaque. A ceremony was held with full military honours and Kelly's descendants – still living in Glasgow – were tracked down and learned for the first time about his heroic deeds.

PROVAN HALL

A hidden medieval gem

80 Auchinlea Road, G34 9NJ
Mon Thurs 9am–4pm, Fri 9am–1.30pm
Free
Easterhouse train station (includes 30-min. walk)
Buses: Stagecoach X19 to Auchinlea Way or any bus towards Easterhouse

Easterhouse is not the kind of place you would traditionally visit, and yet the east end housing scheme is also home to one of Glasgow's hidden medieval gems: Provan Hall.

Once billed as a suburban utopia for city dwellers faced with slum housing and overcrowding, the 1950s housing estate holds a decades-long reputation for poverty and social problems. Glaswegians are slow to forgive the authorities for banishing large numbers of working-class families to a forgotten periphery of the city.

Of course, Glasgow's reputation is often worse than the reality. The same goes for Easterhouse. From the packed Fort shopping centre to community arts venues like Platform, the place is on the up – and you shouldn't be scared to wander off the beaten track into the city's less celebrated east end.

Provan Hall and its surrounding estate (now Auchinlea Park) has a history dating back to 1120, when it was gifted to the church. It was a valuable post, supporting the Prebendary of Barlanark from income derived from the estate, and is said to have been held by at least two illegitimate sons of Stewart kings.

Provan Hall as we know it today dates back to around 1460 and may have been linked to Provand's Lordship in the city centre, the latter acting as a town house for the country estate. Which was built first remains up for debate, but it can be said that Provan Hall is one of (if not the) oldest residences remaining in Glasgow.

The building has had many owners, including Sir Robert Hamilton who acquired it in 1647 (through marriage) and extended it, including the walls to the north and south of the courtyard. He then sold the place to the Burgh of Glasgow, who rented it to five generations of Hamiltons before selling it off in chunks.

By 1934, Provan Hall had long been a working farm but the National Trust for Scotland stepped in and today leases it to the city council, which manages it as a local attraction.

Ghost hunts

Provan Hall holds regular events, including the occasional ghost hunt when thrill-seekers young and old listen to tales of a man with a dagger tearing through the master bedroom, or the spirit of Reston Mather, the estate's last private owner, is often seen on the staircase, still sporting his black bowler hat.

As with any historic site in Scotland, there are even tales of the ghost of Mary Queen of Scots putting in an appearance.

GARTLOCH HOSPITAL

A stunning abandoned insane asylum

Gartloch Road, G69 8EJ
Gartcosh train station

A Victorian insane asylum, long abandoned but with its imposing twin towers still standing ... it sounds like the set of a scary film but, for some Glaswegians, it's home.

Gartloch Hospital grounds closed in 1996, and sections have since been hived off for housing developments, but the A-listed administration building remains untouched; this is the ultimate playground for urban explorers, if they're brave enough.

The east end facility was built in 1889 by John Thomson (the son of Alexander 'Greek' Thomson, no less) and Beaux-Arts-trained Robert Douglas Sandilands, who won the competition for what was then referred to as the City of Glasgow District Asylum.

Today's ruin may conjure up thoughts of Hollywood horror, of escaping mental patients, weird science and the ghosts and ghouls left behind. In fact, the French Renaissance architecture is as imposing as it's distinctive, and even those who are content to wander around the outside will catch glimpses of former grandeur now decaying, brick by brick. The former recreation hall is still famed for its painted ceiling, although those who have ventured close enough say the design is crumbling fast.

There's no shortage of macabre history at Gartloch. The first 500 patients were admitted in 1896. By 1902 it was home to a tuberculosis sanatorium, dealing with the leading cause of death in the western world at the time. Psychiatric patients were housed there until the outbreak of the Second World War, when they were transferred elsewhere to make room for an emergency hospital – huts were erected on the grounds as extra wards, built to cope with demand.

The hospital joined the NHS in 1948 and was a working mental health institution until 1996, when the doors closed for the last time – but not before its Gothic backdrop was given the television treatment. *Doctor Who* fans diving into actor David Tennant's back catalogue may have seen the 1993 BBC series *Takin' Over the Asylum*, about a hospital radio station. Location scouts must have rubbed their hands with glee when they came across Gartloch Hospital.

Today, a new development – Gartloch Village – continues to grow around the old admin building, expanding the village of Gartcosh and providing a green spot to live on the outskirts of Glasgow's east end. Fences surround the old building, deterring anyone walking around Bishop Loch from getting inside and exploring – but many ambitious urban explorers have managed to get a closer look, as numerous pictures and videos online suggest.

Talk of redeveloping the A-listed structure surfaces now and then (at one point, there was even a proposal to turn the old mortuary into a bar) but the site remains derelict, looming over nearby converted flats and no doubt making a perfect party spot when Halloween rolls around.

Thomas Jonglez

It was September 1995 and Thomas Jonglez was in Peshawar, the northern Pakistani city 20 kilometres from the tribal zone he was to visit a few days later. It occurred to him that he should record the hidden aspects of his native city, Paris, which he knew so well. During his seven-month trip back home from Beijing, the countries he crossed took in Tibet (entering clandestinely, hidden under blankets in an overnight bus), Iran and Kurdistan. He never took a plane but travelled by boat, train or bus, hitchhiking, cycling, on horseback or on foot, reaching Paris just in time to celebrate Christmas with the family.

On his return, he spent two fantastic years wandering the streets of the capital to gather material for his first "secret guide", written with a friend. For the next seven years he worked in the steel industry until the passion for discovery overtook him. He launched Jonglez Publishing in 2003 and moved to Venice three years later.

In 2013, in search of new adventures, the family left Venice and spent six months travelling to Brazil, via North Korea, Micronesia, the Solomon Islands, Easter Island, Peru and Bolivia.

After seven years in Rio de Janeiro, he now lives in Berlin with his wife and three children.

Jonglez Publishing produces a range of titles in nine languages, released in 40 countries.

PHOTO BOOKS

Abandoned America
Abandoned Asylums
Abandoned Australia
Abandoned USSR
Abandoned Churches: Unclaimed places of worship
Abandoned cinemas of the world
Abandoned France
Abandoned Italy
Abandoned Japan
Abandoned Spain
After the Final Curtain – The Fall of the American Movie Theater
After the Final Curtain – America's Abandoned Theaters
Baikonur - Vestiges of the Soviet space programme
Chernobyl's Atomic Legacy
Forbidden Places – Exploring our Abandoned Heritage Vol. 1
Forbidden Places – Exploring our Abandoned Heritage Vol. 2
Forbidden Places – Exploring our Abandoned Heritage Vol. 3
Forgotten Heritage
Oblivion
Unusual wines
Venice deserted

'SECRET' GUIDES

New York Hidden bars & restaurants
Secret Amsterdam
Secret Bali – An unusual guide
Secret Bangkok
Secret Barcelona
Secret Belfast
Secret Berlin
Secret Brighton – An unusual guide
Secret Brooklyn
Secret Brussels
Secret Buenos Aires
Secret Campania
Secret Cape Town
Secret Copenhagen
Secret Dublin – An unusual guide
Secret Edinburgh – An unusual guide
Secret Florence
Secret French Riviera
Secret Geneva
Secret Granada
Secret Helsinki
Secret Istanbul
Secret Johannesburg
Secret Lisbon
Secret Liverpool – An unusual guide
Secret London – An unusual guide
Secret London – Unusual bars & restaurants
Secret Madrid
Secret Mexico City
Secret Milan
Secret Montreal – An unusual guide
Secret Naples
Secret New Orleans
Secret New York – An unusual guide
Secret New York – Curious activities
Secret Paris
Secret Prague
Secret Provence
Secret Rio
Secret Rome
Secret Singapore
Secret Sussex – An unusual guide
Secret Tokyo
Secret Tuscany
Secret Venice
Secret Vienna
Secret Washington D.C.
Secret York – An unusual guide

'SOUL OF' GUIDES

Soul of Athens – A guide to 30 exceptional experiences
Soul of Kyoto – A guide to 30 exceptional experiences
Soul of Lisbon – A guide to 30 exceptional experiences
Soul of Los Angeles – A guide to 30 exceptional experiences
Soul of Marrakesh – A guide to 30 exceptional experiences
Soul of New York – A guide to 30 exceptional experiencess
Soul of Rome – A guide to 30 exceptional experiencess
Soul of Tokyo – A guide to 30 exceptional experiences
Soul of Venice – A guide to 30 exceptional experiences

Follow us on Facebook, Instagram and Twitter

ACKNOWLEDGEMENTS

Stephen Millar: My thanks to Kevin Mitchell for helping with the photography for the book, and all the typically generous Glaswegians who helped Gillian and I with queries during the course of putting the book together.

Gillian Loney: Heartfelt thanks to my husband, Chris, and to the Glasgow Live team, who have taught me so much about a city I'm proud to call home.

CREDITS

Photography by **Stephen Millar** and **Kevin Mitchell**, except for :

- Rutherglen Boundary stones: Courtesy of Rutherglen Heritage Society
- Library of Royal Faculty of Procurators in Glasgow: © The Royal Faculty of Procurators in Glasgow

Cartography: Cyrille Suss — **Design:** Emmanuelle Willard Toulemonde — **Editing:** Jana Gough — **Proofreading:** Kimberly Bess — **Publishing:** Clémence Mathé

© JONGLEZ 2022
Registration of copyright: January 2022 - Edition: 01
ISBN: 978-2-36195-357-7
Printed in Slovakia by Polygraf